TOM KiTCHiN
KiTCHiN SUPPERS

PHOTOGRAPHS BY LAURA EDWARDS

Quadrille
PUBLISHING

NOTES

All spoon measures are level unless otherwise stated:

1 teaspoon = 5ml spoon; 1 tablespoon = 15ml spoon.

Use fresh herbs unless otherwise suggested.

Buy unwaxed fruit if you are using the zest.

Timings are for fan-assisted ovens. If you are using a conventional (non-fan) oven, increase the temperature by 15°C (1 Gas mark). Oven temperatures can deviate significantly from the actual setting, so use an oven thermometer to check the temperature.

CONTENTS

INTRODUCTION.

For me, there is nothing more rewarding than enjoying a meal with my family and friends at home. Running The Kitchin, my restaurant in Edinburgh, with my wife Michaela over the past few years has been exciting and challenging. Needless to say, life is pretty hectic most of the time, but home cooking remains an important focus of my life – a chance to relax and share my passion for food with loved ones.

I believe cooking at home should always be fun, never complicated or time-consuming. At home, I love experimenting with dishes that we serve in the restaurant – to create flavourful alternatives that are, above all, intrinsically simple. The secret to successful home cooking is to source good-quality ingredients and to let their flavours shine through, rather than overcomplicate the flavours in a dish. I am as fanatical about seasonality at home as I am in the restaurant, but only because I want everyone to fully appreciate the wonderful natural flavours of fresh produce. If you cook with the seasons, you'll enjoy ingredients at their best and your meals will be naturally varied and interesting throughout the year.

However time-pressured you are, it really is possible to enjoy comforting, home-cooked food throughout the week, as well as at weekends. With just a little forward planning and shopping ahead, you can have a meal on the table within half an hour of coming through the front door. Take my word for it.

Kitchin Suppers is my opportunity to share the food that I cook at home with you. For effortless meals, try my One-pan wonders, Leave it to cook meals and Quick weekday suppers, which can be prepared and cooked in around 30 minutes. If you are entertaining and have a little more time available, you could put together a menu from my Easy starters, Saturday supper and Simple desserts. The Sunday roast chapter – my twists on classic roasts – is particularly close to my heart. The restaurant is closed on Sundays, so it's my chance to enjoy a leisurely day out and about with family and friends, rounded off by a satisfying roast. Throughout the book, I share practical tips on preparing ingredients, cooking techniques and getting the timing right, as well as serving suggestions, to help you along the way.

I hope you will be inspired by Laura Edwards' beautiful photography. Together we prepared and photographed all of the dishes in the book, just as I cook and serve them at home. Whatever the occasion, I'm sure you will find plenty of exciting ideas to tempt you in *Kitchin Suppers*.

Happy Cooking!

ONE-PAN WONDERS

ARTICHOKE BARIGOULE WITH CHORIZO.

This is a phenomenal light supper – easy to prepare in advance, quick to cook and incredibly tasty. The secret to this dish lies in the timing. Have all the ingredients prepared in advance so they can be added at the right moment, without delay. **Serves 4**

6 large artichokes
juice of 2 lemons
olive oil for cooking
250g good-quality chorizo sausages
4 carrots, peeled and sliced
4 shallots, peeled and sliced
2 garlic cloves, peeled and chopped
1 teaspoon coriander seeds
bouquet garni (see page 187)
250ml white wine
about 500ml chicken stock
  (see page 185)
sea salt and freshly ground black
  pepper
1 tablespoon chopped parsley

First prepare the artichokes. Fill a large bowl with cold water and add the juice of 1 lemon. Using a small knife, remove the outer leaves from the artichokes. Now carefully peel away the outer skin from the artichokes and stalk. Cut the artichoke hearts into wedges, removing and discarding the feathery choke at the base. Immediately immerse the artichoke wedges in the lemon water.

Heat a heavy-based frying pan or sauté pan (with a lid). Add a drizzle of olive oil, then the chorizo sausages and cook, stirring, for 2–3 minutes to release the natural oils.

Meanwhile, remove the artichokes from the water and pat dry on kitchen paper. Add them to the pan, put the lid on and sweat gently for 2–3 minutes.

Next add the carrots, shallots, garlic, coriander seeds and bouquet garni. Add the juice of the other lemon and put the lid back on. Sweat together for 2–3 minutes, stirring occasionally; this will release a lot of flavour.

Pour in the white wine and reduce right down until dry, then ladle in enough chicken stock to just cover the ingredients. Simmer, uncovered, for 15 minutes, or until all the vegetables are cooked, adding more stock as it reduces.

Check the seasoning, adding salt and pepper to taste. Scatter over the chopped parsley before serving.

When you peel artichokes, the exposed flesh quickly oxidises and turns brown. Immersing the artichokes in acidulated water as soon as you've prepared each one prevents them from oxidising and discolouring.

SMOKED SALMON, PEA & RED ONION FRITTATA.

Everyone seems to enjoy this quick and easy dish. I often take it along on family picnics, as it tastes just as good when it's cold. Smoked salmon and dill give the frittata distinctive flavours, but you can adapt the recipe to use whatever you happen to have in the fridge. A frittata is a great way to showcase seasonal vegetables – peas and broad beans as here, but also asparagus, baby artichokes, sprouting broccoli and wild mushrooms. And, of course, you can vary the herbs and cheese too. Have fun creating your own versions. **Serves 4**

150g good-quality smoked salmon
2 red onions, peeled
1 courgette
½ large red pepper, cored and
    deseeded
100g freshly podded peas or broad
    beans
8 free-range large eggs
sea salt and freshly ground black
    pepper
1 tablespoon chopped dill
100g Cheddar (ideally locally
    produced), finely grated
olive oil for cooking
snipped chives, to finish

Heat the oven to 160°C/Gas 2–3. Cut the smoked salmon into strips. Cut the red onions, courgette and red pepper into small, even-sized dice.

Add the peas or broad beans to a pan of boiling salted water and blanch for a couple of minutes, then drain and refresh in cold water; drain and pat dry.

In a large bowl, beat the eggs with a fork until lightly foamy. Season with salt and pepper and then add the peas or broad beans, chopped dill, smoked salmon and grated cheese.

Heat a little olive oil in a non-stick (or well-seasoned) ovenproof frying pan, about 23cm in diameter, over a medium heat. Add the onion and cook gently for 2–3 minutes to soften slightly, then add the courgette and red pepper and cook together for2–3 minutes.

Pour the egg mixture over the vegetables in the pan and cook over a low heat for 3–4 minutes. Now transfer the frying pan to the oven and cook for 6–8 minutes until the egg is set and golden on the surface.

Sprinkle the frittata with snipped chives. Cut into portions and serve with a watercress salad.

FISH TRAY BAKE WITH FENNEL & LEMON.

I came up with the idea for this dish several years ago and it's been a family favourite ever since, notably when we are on holiday in the south of France because it's so easily adapted to suit local fish and shellfish. The array of colours is particularly beautiful and enticing. As I prepare ingredients for a recipe and line them up in front of me, I'm often amazed by how lovely they look together… especially with this dish. It's so inspiring. **Serves 4**

2 medallions of monkfish on the bone, about 200g each
2 salmon steaks (middle cut, on the bone), about 170g each
200g mussels in shell
4 raw king or tiger prawns in shell
100g squid with tentacles
extra virgin olive oil for cooking
2 shallots, peeled and sliced
2 garlic cloves, peeled and sliced
1 fennel bulb, trimmed and sliced
1 lemon, sliced
2 tomatoes, sliced
1 bunch of spring onions, trimmed and sliced
sea salt and freshly ground black pepper
100ml white wine
300ml fish stock (see page 185)
50g butter
1 tablespoon fennel seeds
2 basil sprigs
1 tablespoon chopped olives

Heat the oven to 180°C/Gas 4. Have the fish ready at room temperature. Clean the shellfish as necessary, scrubbing the mussels (see page 94), deveining the prawns and separating the squid pouches from the tentacles (see below), unless you've bought ready-cleaned squid.

Oil a large baking tray. Scatter the shallots, garlic, fennel, lemon slices, tomatoes and spring onions on the tray to form a bed and season well with salt and pepper.

Lay the monkfish and salmon on top of the vegetables. Pour over the white wine and fish stock and drizzle over 4–5 tablespoons extra virgin olive oil. Dot the butter on top of the fish and scatter over the fennel seeds. Cover the tray with foil and bake in the oven for 6–8 minutes.

Lift off the foil and add the mussels, prawns and squid to the tray. Re-cover and return to the oven for 8–10 minutes until the fish and shellfish are cooked, basting with the cooking juices from time to time. By now, all the mussels should have opened; discard any that remain closed.

Scatter the basil leaves and chopped olives over the tray bake and serve straight away, with plenty of rustic bread to mop up the delicious juices.

To clean squid, hold the body pouch in one hand and firmly pull the head with your other hand to separate it from the body; the innards will come away too. Remove the quill from the body and peel away the skin. Prise out the beak from the top of the tentacles and cut the tentacles from the head just below the eyes. Rinse the body pouches and tentacles before cooking.

ROASTED MONKFISH WRAPPED IN PANCETTA WITH CHICORY.

Wrapping monkfish in thin slices of pancetta before baking is a great way to protect it from the heat of the oven. The secret is to get the pan really hot before you add the monkfish parcel, so that the pancetta crisps and colours as soon as it hits the pan. In the oven, the fat from the pancetta bastes the fish and prevents it from drying out; it also imparts a wonderful, salty flavour. **Serves 4**

1 filleted monkfish tail, about 450g
2 garlic cloves, peeled
sea salt and freshly ground black
*   pepper*
10–15 thin slices of pancetta
olive oil for cooking
2 chicory bulbs (Belgian endive),
*   halved lengthways*
50g butter
1 tablespoon chopped parsley
1 teaspoon drained small capers

Heat the oven to 180°C/Gas 4. Have the fish ready at room temperature. Halve 1 garlic clove and rub the cut surface all over the monkfish. Season the fish on both sides very lightly with salt (as the pancetta is salty) and with pepper. Set aside.

Next, lay the pancetta slices side by side on a board, overlapping them slightly to form a sheet, the length of the fish. Lay the monkfish across the pancetta and roll the pancetta around it to enclose completely. Secure with kitchen string (see below).

Heat a large non-stick ovenproof frying pan until very hot. Add a drizzle of olive oil and, when it is almost smoking, lay the monkfish parcel in the pan. Cook for 2–3 minutes, turning the parcel to colour all over.

Add the chicory halves to the pan and transfer to the oven. Bake for 6–8 minutes until the monkfish and chicory are cooked.

Meanwhile, chop the other garlic clove for the sauce. To check both the fish and chicory, insert a small knife; it should meet with little resistance. Once cooked, remove the monkfish parcel and chicory from the pan and set aside on a warm plate.

Return the pan to the heat and add the butter, chopped garlic, parsley and capers. Heat gently until melted and bubbling.

Meanwhile, cut the monkfish into 2–3cm slices. Serve with the roasted chicory and caper sauce.

Once you've wrapped the monkfish in the pancetta, tie the parcel at even intervals, taking care not to pull the string too tight; it just needs to hold the parcel together.

CHICKEN & WINTER VEGETABLE BROTH.

This hearty broth is ideal for a quick weekday supper or sustaining lunch. I often make it in the depths of winter, but it is easily transformed into a spring or summer soup with lighter seasonal vegetables, such as courgette, peas and beans in place of leeks and celeriac. The hint of ginger gives a lovely warm, fresh fragrance. **Serves 4**

olive oil for cooking
2 carrots, peeled and diced
½ celeriac, peeled and chopped
2 leeks, trimmed, washed and sliced
1 fennel bulb, trimmed and chopped
1 garlic clove, peeled and finely
   chopped
1 teaspoon finely chopped root ginger
2 free-range boneless chicken breasts,
   about 170g each, skinned and diced
750ml chicken stock (see page 185)
1 bouquet garni (see page 187)
sea salt and freshly ground black
   pepper
50g medium egg noodles
1 tablespoon chopped parsley
2 spring onions, trimmed and sliced

Heat a large heavy-based saucepan over a medium-low heat and add 1–2 tablespoons olive oil. Add the carrots and celeriac and sweat gently for 2–3 minutes, then add the leeks, fennel, garlic and ginger and sweat for a further 2–3 minutes. Now add the diced chicken and stir to combine with the vegetables.

Pour in the chicken stock and bring to a simmer. Add the bouquet garni and some salt and pepper. Simmer the broth gently for 12 minutes.

Drop the egg noodles into the stock and cook for a further 5 minutes or until the noodles are cooked through. Taste and adjust the seasoning.

Scatter the chopped parsley and sliced spring onions over the broth to serve.

If you've had roast chicken for Sunday lunch and have some meat left over, this is an ideal recipe to prepare for lunch early on in the week. Strip the meat from the carcass, wrap it in cling film and refrigerate until ready to prepare the soup. Use the carcass to make chicken stock (following the recipe on page 185). When you make the soup, dice the leftover chicken and add it with the noodles, just to heat through.

LEMON & GARLIC ROASTED GUINEA FOWL WITH SAUTÉED POTATOES.

The flavours complement each other beautifully in this dish. I love the mild gamey taste of guinea fowl, but a good free-range chicken will also work very well here. Sautéeing the potatoes in the fat from the guinea fowl infuses them with the flavour of the bird. As an added bonus, once you've removed the breasts and legs from the bird, you have a fresh carcass to make stock with. **Serves 4**

1 free-range guinea fowl, about 1.2kg
olive oil for marinating and cooking
sea salt and freshly ground black
   pepper
1 tablespoon dried herbes de Provence
2 fennel bulbs, trimmed
500g baby new potatoes (ideally
   similar in size), washed and
   patted dry
1 teaspoon caraway seeds
½ head of garlic (cut horizontally)
1 lemon, halved or cut into wedges
2 thyme sprigs
2 baby gem lettuces, halved
   lengthways
25g unsalted butter, in pieces

Heat the oven to 180°C/Gas 4. To make it easier to cut the breasts from the bird, first remove the wishbone. To do this, cut down either side of the wishbone with a sharp knife, then reach in with your fingers and hook the bone out. Cut the breasts and legs from the guinea fowl carcass and put them into a dish. Drizzle with olive oil, season with salt and pepper, and sprinkle with the dried herbs. Leave to sit for 10 minutes.

Meanwhile, cut each fennel bulb into 6 wedges. Cut any larger baby potatoes in half.

Heat a large heavy-based ovenproof frying pan over a medium heat and add 1 tablespoon olive oil. When hot, add the guinea fowl legs and breasts to the pan, placing them skin side down. Cook for 5–6 minutes until they start to take on a nice golden colour, then turn and do the same on the other side. Remove the guinea fowl pieces to a plate and set aside.

Return the frying pan to the heat and add a little more olive oil if needed. Tip the potatoes into the pan and season with salt and pepper. Sauté for 2–3 minutes, then add the fennel and cook for a further 2–3 minutes. Scatter over the caraway seeds and add the garlic, lemon and thyme.

Place the guinea fowl on top of the vegetables, cover the pan with a lid and cook in the oven for 10–12 minutes.

Remove the guinea fowl breasts to a warm plate, cover and set aside to rest in a warm place. Give the potatoes, fennel and guinea fowl legs a stir, put the lid back on and return to the oven for a further 12–15 minutes until cooked. Add the lettuce, dot with the butter, cover and cook for a further 2 minutes.

Place the guinea fowl breasts back on top of the potatoes and fennel and serve.

RUMP OF LAMB WITH A RAGOUT OF PEAS, CARROTS & LETTUCE.

To me, rump has more flavour than other prime cuts of lamb and this way of cooking it really maximises the taste. The vegetable ragout is my tweak on *petits pois à la française*. Cooking the vegetables in the pan used for the lamb and lardons infuses them with the lovely, intense flavours to delicious effect.

Serves 4

4 rumps of lamb, about 180–200g each
sea salt and freshly ground black
  pepper
olive oil for cooking
100g bacon lardons or pancetta,
  cut into strips
2 carrots, peeled and finely diced
500g freshly podded peas
150–200ml chicken stock
  (see page 185)
1 baby gem lettuce, thinly sliced
25g unsalted butter, in pieces

Heat the oven to 180°C/Gas 4. Season the lamb rumps on both sides with salt and pepper and set aside to rest for 10 minutes.

Heat an ovenproof frying pan over a medium-high heat and add a little olive oil. When hot, add the rumps of lamb and turn to colour well all over.

Transfer the pan to the oven and cook for a further 5–6 minutes for medium-rare lamb. Once cooked, transfer the lamb to a warm plate and set aside in a warm place to rest.

Return the pan to the heat, add a little more olive oil, then the lardons. Cook for 1–2 minutes until the lardons start to colour (and release their salty flavour). Add the carrots and cook for a further 2–3 minutes. Then add the peas, stir and season.

Pour on enough chicken stock to just cover and cook over a high heat for 3–4 minutes, adding more stock as needed. Once the peas are cooked, stir through the lettuce and butter.

Slice the rumps of lamb and serve them on the bed of vegetables and lardons.

PORK FILLET WITH SAUTÉED APPLE, BLACK PUDDING & CALVADOS SAUCE.

I love pork in all its different guises, but this recipe is a particular favourite of mine. Pork and apple are traditionally paired, but I'm adding a twist here by including some black pudding and serving the dish with a creamy Calvados sauce. Use good-quality free-range pork for optimum flavour and take care to avoid overcooking, which quickly toughens and dries the meat. **Serves 4**

4 pork fillet (tenderloin) pieces, about 160–170g each
sea salt and freshly cracked black pepper
olive oil for cooking
2 crisp, green-skinned dessert apples
4 slices of good-quality black pudding, about 50g each
50g butter
100ml Calvados
250ml whipping cream

Heat the oven to 180°C/Gas 4. Season the pork fillets with salt and cracked pepper. Heat a non-stick ovenproof frying pan over a medium-high heat and add a little olive oil. When hot, add the pork fillets and cook for 2–3 minutes, turning to colour all over.

Transfer the pan to the oven for 5–6 minutes to finish cooking the pork. In the meantime, cut each apple into 6 wedges and remove the core; set aside.

When the pork is cooked through, transfer it to a warm plate and set aside in a warm place to rest.

Meanwhile, return the pan to the heat, add the black pudding slices and fry for 2–3 minutes on each side until cooked. Remove from the pan and place with the pork.

Now add the butter to the pan, allow to melt and then add the apples. Sauté for 3–4 minutes. Now add the Calvados and flambé, standing well back and using a long match to set the alcohol alight. Once the flame had subsided, let the liquor bubble to reduce right down, then remove the apples with a slotted spoon and add them to the pork.

Pour the cream into the pan, bring to the boil and season with a little salt and pepper. Reduce again, until thickened to the required consistency. Taste and adjust the seasoning as necessary.

Slice the pork fillets and arrange on warm plates with the black pudding. Pour on the creamy sauce and finish with the sautéed apple wedges.

SAUSAGE & BUTTER BEAN CASSEROLE.

This is the ultimate fast supper – one that kids love too. I sometimes need to rustle up a dinner for the family without time to shop or prepare ingredients and this simple recipe is the ideal solution, as it's based on things that I usually have in the fridge or freezer. It's one of those dishes that tastes almost as good the next day, so if you have any left over, keep it in the fridge or freeze it for another day. **Serves 4**

olive or sunflower oil for cooking
6 good-quality sausages
4 rashers of bacon, derinded and cut
  into strips
1 white onion, peeled and chopped
1 garlic clove, peeled and chopped
1 teaspoon dried herbes de Provence
2 x 400g tins butter beans, rinsed
400g tin chopped tomatoes
200ml chicken stock (see page 185)
sea salt and freshly ground black
  pepper

Herby crumb topping
150g white bread (ideally day old),
  crusts removed
50g parsley, roughly chopped
50g tarragon, roughly chopped
50g chervil, roughly chopped

Heat the oven to 200°C/Gas 6. Heat a heavy-based ovenproof sauté pan or shallow flameproof casserole and add a drizzle of oil. Once hot, add the sausages and cook, turning, for a few minutes to colour evenly. Add the bacon strips and cook for a further 3–4 minutes.

Add the onion with the garlic and dried herbs and cook for 5 minutes to soften, stirring from time to time.

Meanwhile, for the herby crumb topping, tear the breadcrumbs into chunks and put into a blender with the herbs. Blitz until the bread is reduced to crumbs and the herbs are finely chopped.

Add the butter beans, tomatoes and chicken stock to the pan, stir to mix everything together and season well with salt and pepper. Sprinkle the herby crumbs evenly over the surface and bake for 25 minutes until the topping is crisp. Serve with a leafy salad for contrast if you like.

QUICK WEEKDAY SUPPERS

RISOTTO WITH GARLIC, GIROLLES, PARSLEY & CRISPY PARMA HAM.

A freshly cooked risotto can be absolutely delicious and takes only around 18 minutes to prepare, from start to finish. To me, it's a dish that really benefits from love and concentration as you make it: stir and taste as you go, adjust the seasoning as necessary and look for that lovely creamy texture and *al dente* bite to the rice that tell you the risotto is ready. It's not a dish to prepare ahead. **Serves 4**

800ml chicken stock (see page 185)
100g butter
1 white onion, peeled and finely chopped
sea salt and freshly ground black pepper
250g risotto rice
100ml white wine
olive oil for cooking
8 slices of Parma ham
250g girolles, cleaned
2 garlic cloves, peeled and chopped
2 tablespoons chopped parsley
100g Parmesan, freshly grated, plus extra shavings to serve

Bring the chicken stock to the boil in a saucepan and keep it at a low simmer.

In another heavy-based saucepan, melt 50g of the butter, add the onion and sweat for 3–4 minutes to soften without colouring. Season with salt and pepper. Add the rice and stir to coat the grains in the butter. Cook for 1 minute, then pour in the white wine and let bubble to reduce right down.

Now start adding the stock, a ladleful (50–100ml) at a time, stirring and allowing each addition to be fully absorbed before adding the next. Continue to add the stock in this way until the rice is *al dente* (cooked but with a slight bite); this will take 15–17 minutes.

Meanwhile, heat a large non-stick frying pan over a medium-high heat and add a little olive oil. Fry the Parma ham in batches as necessary until crispy; remove and set aside.

Heat a little more oil in the pan and add the girolles with some seasoning. Cook over a medium-high heat for 1–2 minutes until tender; remove with a slotted spoon and set aside. Drain the liquid from the pan into the risotto.

Wipe the frying pan clean, add a little more oil and sauté the chopped garlic for a minute. Remove from the heat, add the crispy Parma ham slices, girolles and chopped parsley and set aside, ready for serving.

Once the risotto is cooked, remove the pan from the heat. Add the grated Parmesan and remaining 50g butter, in pieces, and fork through.

Divide the risotto between warm serving bowls and top with the girolles, crispy Parma ham, parsley and garlic. Finish with a few shavings of Parmesan.

KEDGEREE.

This is a lovely light, tasty supper, but it's also a brilliant brunch dish. Quick to make and just as easy to prepare double or triple the quantity, it's an ideal dish for a larger gathering. We often have this kedgeree at Christmas and Easter, but also on other occasions throughout the year when we have family and friends staying. **Serves 4**

600g smoked haddock fillets
  (with skin)
2 garlic cloves, peeled
600ml milk
50g butter
½ onion, peeled and finely chopped
½ teaspoon curry powder
½ teaspoon white mustard seeds
sea salt and freshly ground black
  pepper
.200g basmati rice
500ml water
4 free-range medium eggs
juice of ½ lemon, to taste
2 tablespoons chopped parsley
lime or lemon wedges, to serve

Put the smoked haddock into a wide pan, add the garlic cloves and pour on the milk to cover. Lay a round of baking parchment or buttered greaseproof paper on top and place over a very low heat. Bring up to a gentle simmer and turn off the heat, leaving the smoked haddock to finish cooking in the residual heat for a minute or two.

Lift out the cooked fish onto a board, reserving the liquor. Flake the smoked haddock, cover with cling film and set aside.

Melt the butter in a heavy-based saucepan. Add the onion and sprinkle with the curry powder, mustard seeds and some salt and pepper. Sweat gently, stirring frequently, for 5 minutes to soften. Add the rice and stir to coat with the butter.

Pour the water and 100ml of the reserved poaching milk over the rice, bring to the boil and then simmer for about 15 minutes until the rice is cooked and the liquid has evaporated.

Meanwhile, boil the eggs in water to cover for 8 minutes, then drain and refresh under cold running water. Shell the hard-boiled eggs and cut into wedges.

Add the smoked haddock to the rice, gently fold through and season with lemon juice, salt and pepper to taste. Add the chopped hard-boiled eggs and scatter over the chopped parsley. Serve with lime or lemon wedges.

GRILLED HADDOCK WITH SPINACH & TARTARE SAUCE.

Haddock takes no longer than 5 minutes to cook under the grill – perfect for a fast supper and delicious with a chunky tartare sauce. A good-quality bought mayonnaise will do for the base if you haven't any homemade mayo in the fridge. Spinach is excellent with grilled fish – try sautéeing it my way. **Serves 4**

75g butter
4 haddock fillets, skinned, about
*   150g each*
sea salt and freshly ground black
*   pepper*
50ml white wine
juice of 1 lemon
olive oil for cooking
200g spinach, washed
1 garlic clove, peeled (optional)
1 tablespoon chopped parsley
4 lemon slices, to finish

Tartare sauce

200ml good-quality mayonnaise
*   (ideally homemade, see page 187)*
50g gherkins, chopped
50g shallots, peeled and chopped
50g capers, rinsed and chopped
2 tablespoons chopped parsley

First make the tartare sauce. Mix the mayonnaise with the gherkins, shallots, capers and parsley. Season with pepper to taste (the capers should provide enough salt). Transfer to a small serving dish, cover and set aside until ready to serve.

Heat the grill to medium. Line the grill tray with foil and smear with a little of the butter. Place the haddock on the buttered foil and season with a little salt. Sprinkle the fish fillets with the white wine and lemon juice and dot with the rest of the butter. Place under the grill for 4–5 minutes until cooked.

Meanwhile, heat a frying pan and add a little olive oil. Add the spinach and sauté briefly (see below) until just wilted. Season with salt and pepper to taste.

Once the fish is cooked, scatter over the chopped parsley and top with the lemon slices.

Carefully lift the haddock fillets onto warm plates. Tip the cooking juices into a small pan, reheat if necessary and trickle over the fish. Serve with the wilted spinach and tartare sauce.

Rather than cook spinach in the usual way – in a covered pan with the minimum of water – I like to sauté it briefly in olive oil, lending a subtle garlic flavour at the same time. To do this, spear a peeled garlic clove on a fork. Heat a frying pan with a little olive oil, add the spinach, season with a little salt and toss with the fork until just wilted. This takes less than a minute and gives the spinach a mild garlic flavour, which is just beautiful.

ROASTED HAKE WITH CHICKPEA, FETA & RED ONION SALAD.

Hake has become increasingly popular in the UK in recent years, as we've turned to more sustainable fish as an alternative to threatened species. I use hake a lot in my restaurant, but also at home. This is a lovely comfort dish with enticing Moroccan flavours. If you happen to have a batch of home-cooked chickpeas in the fridge or freezer, this is a good way to use them, but good-quality tinned chickpeas are perfectly acceptable for the salad. **Serves 4**

4 portions of hake (with skin), about
  130g each
sea salt and freshly ground black
  pepper
olive oil for cooking

Chickpea, feta and red onion salad
400g tin chickpeas, drained
1 red onion, peeled and thinly sliced
100–120g feta, cut into cubes
125g cherry tomatoes
extra virgin olive oil to drizzle
1 teaspoon sherry vinegar
1 tablespoon chopped black olives
1 tablespoon chopped basil
100g chorizo, thinly sliced

Heat the oven to 180°C/Gas 4. Season the hake portions on both sides with salt and pepper and set aside.

For the salad, put the chickpeas into a large bowl with the red onion, feta cubes, cherry tomatoes and a good drizzle of extra virgin olive oil. Add the sherry vinegar, chopped olives and basil. Toss to mix and season with salt and pepper to taste. Set aside.

Heat a large non-stick ovenproof frying pan over a medium-high heat. When it is hot, add a little olive oil and place the hake portions in the pan, skin side down. Cook, without moving, for 2–3 minutes. Now place the pan in the oven for 3–4 minutes until the fish is cooked.

Meanwhile, divide the chickpea salad between plates. Place the hake portions, skin side up, on top and scatter the sliced chorizo over the salad.

Achieving a crispy skin on fish is a bit of an art. The secret is to make sure the skin is dry, and to use a non-stick ovenproof frying pan. Get your pan really hot before placing the fish, skin side down, in it. Shake the pan gently but don't try to move the fish around with a spatula, otherwise it is liable to stick. Finishing the cooking in the oven enables the flesh side to cook through without becoming dry.

SMOKED MACKEREL SALAD WITH HONEY MUSTARD DRESSING.

Mackerel is one of my all-time favourite fish and one of the few that I have managed to catch myself off the west coast of Scotland. I enjoy mixing and matching it with different ingredients through the seasons, not least new potatoes in the summer. Mackerel is popular in Scandinavian cooking and my Swedish wife Michaela was the inspiration for this recipe. I love its simplicity and uncomplicated fresh flavours. Michaela's Swedish honey mustard dressing marries the summery flavours perfectly. **Serves 4**

600g baby new potatoes
sea salt and freshly ground black
  pepper
4 free-range medium eggs
4 smoked mackerel fillets, about
  100g each
1 avocado
1 red onion, peeled and sliced
4 baby gem lettuce, halved lengthways
250g cherry tomatoes, halved
olive oil to drizzle
4 cooked beetroot, sliced

Honey mustard dressing
2 tablespoons Dijon mustard
2 teaspoons caster sugar
2 teaspoons white wine vinegar
150ml vegetable oil
2 teaspoons chopped dill

First make the dressing. Mix the mustard, sugar, wine vinegar and some salt and pepper together in a medium bowl. Now slowly add the oil, whisking or stirring vigorously as you do so to emulsify and thicken the sauce (an electric hand whisk is ideal for this). Stir in the chopped dill and set aside.

Cook the baby potatoes in boiling salted water for 12–15 minutes until just tender. Meanwhile, boil the eggs in water to cover for 8 minutes.

Once the potatoes are cooked, drain and thickly slice them. When the eggs are cooked, drain and refresh under cold running water, then peel and cut in half.

Break the smoked mackerel fillets into big chunks. Halve, stone and peel the avocado, then cut into slices.

Put the potatoes into a large bowl with the red onion, lettuce, cherry tomatoes and avocado. Season with salt and pepper to taste and drizzle with a little olive oil. Toss gently to mix.

Divide the beetroot, dressed salad and smoked mackerel between plates and add the hard-boiled egg halves. Spoon over the honey mustard dressing, grind over some pepper and serve.

SALMON WITH 'BEURRE D'ESCARGOT' & SPINACH.

Beurre d'escargot is a delicious savoury butter traditionally paired with snails, though in the restaurant we more often serve it with lobster. Here I am using it with salmon, a meaty fish that can take the salty ham and garlic flavours well. It is also good with other meaty fish, beef steaks and chicken. Freeze any of the butter that you don't need for the salmon, wrapped in cling film, and slice it from frozen whenever you want to use it. **Serves 4**

4 salmon fillets (with skin), about
   150g each
sea salt and freshly ground black
   pepper
olive oil for cooking
300g baby spinach
squeeze of lemon juice, to taste

Beurre d'escargot
2 teaspoons olive oil
25g Parma ham, finely chopped
1 shallot, peeled and finely chopped
50g fennel, trimmed and finely
   chopped
50g button mushrooms, finely
   chopped
1 garlic clove, peeled and crushed
1 teaspoon chopped parsley
1 tablespoon chopped tarragon
250g butter, softened
1 tablespoon grain mustard
1 tablespoon ground almonds

To serve
lemon wedges

First make the savoury butter. Heat a large non-stick frying pan over a medium-high heat, then add a little olive oil. Add the chopped Parma ham to the pan and cook for 2 minutes, stirring occasionally. Now add the shallot, fennel, mushrooms and garlic with the rest of the olive oil and sweat for 3–4 minutes, stirring occasionally. Add the chopped herbs, stir well, then remove from the heat and let cool.

In a separate bowl, whisk the butter until creamy. Add the cooled vegetables and ham and stir to combine. Now add the mustard and ground almonds and mix well. Spoon the butter onto a sheet of cling film and roll it in the cling film to form a log. Twist the ends to secure. Refrigerate to firm up.

When ready to serve, heat the oven to 180°C/Gas 4. Season the salmon fillets on both sides with salt and pepper. Heat a large non-stick ovenproof frying pan over a medium-high heat. When it is hot, add a little olive oil and place the salmon fillets in the pan, skin side down. Cook, without moving, for 2–3 minutes until the skin starts to crisp. Now place the pan in the oven for 3–4 minutes until the fish is cooked.

In the meantime, unwrap the savoury butter and cut 4 generous slices. When the salmon is cooked, transfer the fillets to a warm plate and set aside in a warm place. Heat a little more oil in the frying pan, add the spinach, season and toss briefly until wilted. Remove from the heat and add lemon juice to taste.

Divide the spinach between warm plates and lay a salmon fillet across the middle. Top with a slice of savoury butter and serve with lemon wedges.

CHAR-GRILLED CHICKEN, SUMMER VEGETABLES & CROÛTONS WITH BLUE CHEESE DRESSING.

This dish is all about summer, fresh flavours and simple eating. The blue cheese dressing brings the elements together perfectly. It's versatile too – I use it to dress a variety of salads and as a dip for summer vegetable crudités. **Serves 4**

*2 free-range boneless chicken breasts
with skin, about 170g each*
olive oil for cooking
*sea salt and freshly ground black
pepper*
few rosemary sprigs
*2 fennel bulbs, trimmed and cut into
wedges*
*8 asparagus spears, woody bases
snapped off and lower stalks peeled*
1 courgette, sliced
½ baguette
1 garlic clove, halved
*3–4 baby gem lettuces, halved or
quartered*
*1 bunch of radishes, trimmed and
halved*
12 cherry tomatoes, halved

Blue cheese dressing
50g blue cheese
100ml mayonnaise (see page 187)
50g crème fraîche

Heat the oven to 180°C/Gas 4 and heat up a griddle. Put the chicken into a bowl, drizzle with olive oil and season with salt and pepper. Break up the rosemary sprigs, add to the bowl and toss everything together.

To prepare the dressing, in a bowl, break up the blue cheese with a fork. Add the mayonnaise and crème fraîche and mix until smoothly combined.

Place the chicken on the hot griddle, skin side down, and cook, without turning for 6–8 minutes. In the meantime, toss the fennel, asparagus and courgette separately in a little olive oil.

Once the chicken has been cooking for 8 minutes, add the vegetables to the griddle in the following order: first the fennel, then after 2 minutes the asparagus, then after another 2 minutes the courgette. Cook the vegetables and chicken together, turning as necessary; the whole process should take 16–18 minutes. Once cooked, remove from the griddle and set aside.

Meanwhile, for the croûtons, cut the baguette into chunks, drizzle with olive oil and rub with the cut garlic clove. Place the chunks of bread on a baking tray and bake for 6–8 minutes until golden, turning occasionally.

To serve, divide the lettuce, radishes, tomatoes and char-grilled chicken and vegetables between serving plates. Season with salt and pepper, drizzle with olive oil and toss lightly. Scatter the croûtons over the salad, spoon on the dressing and serve.

CHICKEN & BROCCOLI BAKE.

This simple midweek supper takes me back to my childhood as it's an adaptation of one of my mother's recipes. If I have time I'll poach a whole chicken rather than chicken breasts, as it gives a tastier stock.
Serves 4

4 free-range boneless chicken breasts, skinned, about 150g each
700ml water
1 onion, peeled and quartered
1 carrot, peeled and sliced
bouquet garni (see page 187)
5 black peppercorns
sea salt and freshly ground black pepper
1 head of broccoli, cut into florets
50g butter
50g plain flour
1 teaspoon ground cumin
1 tablespoon curry powder
1 tablespoon crème fraîche
100g Cheddar, grated
squeeze of lemon juice, to taste
50g fresh white breadcrumbs (ideally day old)
1–2 tablespoons roughly chopped flat-leaf parsley, to finish

Heat the oven to 180°C/Gas 4. Have the chicken breasts ready at room temperature.

Bring the water to the boil in a wide pan. Add the onion, carrot, bouquet garni and peppercorns and simmer for 10 minutes. Add the chicken breasts, making sure there is enough water to cover them. Lower the heat and poach gently for 10–12 minutes. Remove from the heat.

Using a slotted spoon, lift out the chicken and vegetables onto a plate and set aside. Measure 600ml stock and reserve.

In another pan of boiling salted water, blanch the broccoli for 3–4 minutes. Drain and set aside.

Meanwhile, heat the butter in a heavy-based saucepan, stir in the flour and cook for 1–2 minutes. Now add the cumin and curry powder and cook, stirring frequently, for another 2 minutes. Gradually stir in the reserved stock and bring to the boil, stirring.

Let the sauce simmer, stirring often, for 4 minutes, then remove from the heat. Stir in the crème fraîche and grated Cheddar. Add a squeeze of lemon juice and season with salt and pepper to taste.

Tear or cut the chicken into pieces. Scatter the reserved onion and carrot into a buttered, shallow ovenproof dish. Add the chicken and broccoli florets.

Pour the cheese sauce over the chicken and vegetables to cover. Sprinkle with the breadcrumbs and bake for 20–25 minutes until the topping is golden brown and crunchy. Scatter the chopped parsley over the bake and serve.

RIB-EYE STEAK WITH SHALLOT & PARSLEY MARMALADE.

Friends tell me they enjoy cooking a steak for supper, but can't seem to make a good sauce to go with it. In truth, it's almost impossible to match the depth of flavour achieved by the lengthy reduction of sauces in a restaurant kitchen. So, I experimented at home and came up with this shallot and parsley topping. I think it's delicious and works as well as any sauce. And I love the fact that the entire meal can be on the table within 30 minutes of coming home, if you have the ingredients to hand. **Serves 4**

4 rib-eye steaks, about 250g each
olive oil for cooking
12 shallots, peeled and sliced
sea salt and freshly ground black
* pepper*
250ml white wine
1 teaspoon cracked black pepper
1 tablespoon grain mustard
2 tablespoons chopped parsley

Remove the steaks from the fridge, ideally 20 minutes before you need to cook them, to bring to room temperature.

Heat a heavy-based saucepan and add a drizzle of olive oil. Add the shallots, season with salt and pepper and sweat gently for 4–5 minutes. Pour in half the white wine and reduce right down until dry, then repeat with the rest of the wine. Remove from the heat and set aside until ready to use.

Meanwhile, heat a heavy-based, non-stick frying pan over a high heat. Season the steaks well with salt and the cracked pepper. When the pan is very hot, add a little drizzle of olive oil, then the steaks. Colour them quickly, for 4–5 minutes on each side, depending on how rare you like your meat, lowering the heat to medium after a couple of minutes on each side.

Remove the steaks from the pan to a warmed platter and set aside to rest in a warm place for 5 minutes before serving.

While the steaks are resting, return the frying pan to a medium heat and add the cooked shallots, mustard and chopped parsley. Cook for 1–2 minutes and serve on top or alongside the steaks.

Knowing when a steak is cooked just by pressing it comes naturally after so many years, but if you are unsure, the thumb trick is a great indicator. Open the palm of your right hand and relax the hand. Take the left hand and push the skin area by the base of the right thumb to see how raw meet feels. Now press your right thumb and little fingertip together and you'll feel that skin area harden: this feels like well done meat. To simulate the feel of medium, press the thumb and ring fingertip together. For rare, press the thumb and index finger together; the skin area should give quite a bit and be a lot softer. Now press your steak to check that it is cooked to your liking.

PORK CHOPS WITH TOMATO COMPOTE & GRILLED CHEDDAR.

The difference between good-quality pork and standard pork is as huge as the difference between free-range and battery-farmed chickens in my view, so I'd recommend shopping carefully, seeking out rare-breed or at least organic pork if possible. Here the chops are pan-fried, then topped with a fresh tomato compote and cheese and finished under the grill. Overcooked pork is rubbery and unpleasant to eat, so it is vital to buy chops of the right thickness and to get the timing right. **Serves 4**

4 pork chops, about 180g each
   and 2.5–3cm thick
sea salt and freshly ground black
   pepper
olive oil for cooking

Tomato compote
2 shallots, peeled and sliced
1 garlic clove, peeled and chopped
6 tomatoes, chopped
2 spring onions, trimmed and
   thinly sliced
1 teaspoon chopped black olives
1 teaspoon chopped basil

To serve
180–200g Cheddar, sliced

For the tomato compote, heat a wide heavy-based saucepan and add a little olive oil. Add the shallots with some salt and pepper and sweat gently for 3–4 minutes without colouring. Now add the garlic and tomatoes and sweat for 2–3 minutes.

Put a lid on the pan and cook for a further 6–8 minutes (the tomatoes will release a lot of their liquid during this time). Remove the lid and let bubble for 10–12 minutes to reduce the liquid until you have a compote consistency.

Meanwhile, heat the grill to medium-high. Heat a large non-stick frying pan over a medium-high heat and season the pork chops with salt and pepper. Add a drizzle of olive oil to the hot frying pan and place the chops in the pan. Colour for 2–3 minutes on each side. Remove from the pan and place in a large gratin dish.

Next, stir the spring onions, olives and basil into the tomato compote and spread on top of the chops. Lay the Cheddar slices on top and place under the grill for 3–4 minutes until melted and bubbling. Serve with French beans and/or a leafy salad.

FOUR CHEESE OMELETTE WITH COURGETTE.

When time is short, this omelette is a real winner as it is incredibly quick to put together. Vary the cheeses according to what you happen to have to hand – I like to use local varieties and this is a good opportunity to see how their flavours complement each other. And, of course, you can use other vegetables in season, such as asparagus, broad beans or peas, for the filling. **Serves 1**

3 free-range medium eggs
sea salt and freshly ground black
  pepper
½ courgette, sliced, or a handful of
  broccoli florets
olive oil for cooking
1 teaspoon butter
50g mixed finely grated Gruyère,
  Cheddar, Parmesan and blue cheese,
  such as Lanark Blue (or Stilton)
4 cherry tomatoes, halved or
  quartered
1 tablespoon chopped parley

In a bowl, lightly whisk the eggs and season with salt and pepper. Blanch the courgette slices or broccoli florets briefly in a pan of boiling salted water for 2 minutes until just tender. Drain and refresh under cold water; drain thoroughly.

Heat a 20cm non-stick frying pan. When the pan is hot, add a drizzle of olive oil and then the butter. Pour in the beaten eggs and allow to cook for about 20 seconds until the egg starts to set on the bottom. Now, to ensure the omelette cooks evenly, gently push the cooked egg from the edge towards the middle using a wooden spoon, to allow the uncooked egg to run out to the edge of the pan. The omelette will take 1½–2 minutes to cook.

Sprinkle the four cheeses, tomatoes, courgette or broccoli and chopped parsley evenly over the surface of the omelette. Run a spatula around the edge of the omelette to make sure it is not sticking, and shake the pan a little to check that the underside moves freely.

Now fold the omelette in half to enclose the filling. The easiest way to do this is to tilt the pan and then flick one side on top of the other. Slide the omelette out of the pan onto a plate. Serve with a green salad.

ROASTED PUMPKIN, JERUSALEM ARTICHOKES & BEETROOT WITH HAZELNUT DRESSING.

Nuts go well with roasted vegetables and I'll often scatter a handful of toasted nuts over a tray of roasted veg before serving, although I sometimes choose to use a nut dressing instead. The hazelnut oil in this dressing intensifies the nutty taste and moistens the vegetables. It's a versatile dressing too – equally delicious over grilled fish or shellfish, or used to dress a simple crab salad or French beans. **Serves 4**

2 beetroot
sea salt and freshly ground black
  pepper
4 Jerusalem artichokes
juice of ½ lemon
1kg pumpkin
olive oil for cooking

Hazelnut dressing
50g hazelnuts, roughly chopped
2 shallots, peeled and finely chopped
1 tablespoon chopped chives
50ml hazelnut oil
1 teaspoon sherry vinegar, or to taste

To finish
handful of watercress sprigs

Heat the oven to 180°C/Gas 4. Peel the beetroot, wearing plastic gloves to avoid staining your hands red. Cut into quarters, place in a saucepan and pour on enough water to cover. Add salt and bring to the boil. Simmer for 30 minutes or until the beetroot is about three-quarters cooked. Drain and set aside.

Meanwhile, peel the Jerusalem artichokes, cut them in half and immerse in a bowl of cold water with the lemon juice added to stop them discolouring. Peel away the skin from the pumpkin and remove the seeds. Cut into thick moon-shaped slices.

Heat a large non-stick ovenproof frying pan (or a cast-iron roasting pan) over a medium-high heat and add a drizzle of olive oil. Place the pumpkin and Jerusalem artichokes in the pan, season with salt and cook for 3–4 minutes, turning to colour. Transfer to the oven and roast for 15 minutes.

Cut the beetroot into wedges, add to the pan and cook in the oven for a further 5 minutes.

Meanwhile, make the dressing. Combine the chopped hazelnuts, shallots, chives and hazelnut oil in a bowl. Add a splash of sherry vinegar and season with salt and pepper to taste.

Spoon the dressing over the roasted vegetables and scatter over the watercress to serve.

LEAVE IT TO COOK

SMOKED SALMON & SPINACH LASAGNE.

This comforting pasta bake is easy to prepare and always popular. The recipe is based on a Scandinavian dish that my wife Michaela has been making for years. It's absolutely delicious and has the added advantage that it can be prepared in advance, ready to bake and serve when required. **Serves 4–6**

Béchamel sauce
75g butter
75g plain flour
850ml milk
sea salt and freshly ground black
 pepper

Lasagne
25g butter
1 leek, trimmed, washed and cut
 into strips
400g baby spinach
2 garlic cloves, peeled and crushed
400g smoked salmon
300g Cheddar, grated
8–10 lasagne sheets
4 dill sprigs, roughly chopped,
 to garnish

Heat the oven to 180°C/Gas 4. To make the béchamel sauce, melt the butter in a heavy-based saucepan, stir in the flour and cook for 1–2 minutes. Slowly stir in the milk and cook at a gentle simmer, stirring frequently, until the sauce thickens. Season with salt and pepper to taste. Set aside.

For the lasagne, melt half the butter in a heavy-based pan over a medium-low heat. Add the leek strips, season with salt and pepper and sweat gently for 2–3 minutes. Add the spinach leaves, a handful at a time, along with the garlic and cook for another minute or two. Drain off the excess liquid.

Use the rest of the butter to grease a large square or rectangular ovenproof dish. Cut the smoked salmon into small pieces, roughly 2cm square.

Spoon a layer of the béchamel sauce over the bottom of the dish and layer a third of the lasagne sheets on top. Spoon half of the leek and spinach mixture over the lasagne, followed by a good third of the smoked salmon, then cover with a third of the remaining béchamel and sprinkle some cheese over the surface. Repeat the layers of lasagne, leek and spinach, smoked salmon, béchamel and cheese, then cover with a top layer of lasagne.

Spoon the rest of the béchamel sauce on top and scatter over the remaining smoked salmon and grated cheese. Bake for about 45 minutes until the top is a deep golden colour. To check that the lasagne is cooked, insert a knife in the middle; it should meet with minimal resistance.

Scatter the chopped dill on top of the lasagne and serve, with a crisp green salad on the side.

BRAISED DUCK LEG WITH ORANGE, OLIVES & BASIL.

I love the rustic flavours in this simple braise, and polenta is a great accompaniment as it soaks up the tasty braising liquor. Duck legs are ideal for braising – you just need to keep an eye on them to ensure they don't overcook, otherwise the meat will simply fall away from the bone. **Serves 4**

4 large duck legs
plain flour for dusting
sea salt and freshly ground black
  pepper
olive oil for cooking
2 carrots, peeled and chopped
½ celeriac, peeled and chopped
½ onion, peeled and chopped
bouquet garni (see page 187)
finely pared zest and juice of 2 oranges
75cl bottle of red wine
10g butter
1 tablespoon chopped olives
1 tablespoon chopped basil

Polenta
500ml milk
freshly grated nutmeg
10g butter
200g fine polenta

Heat the oven to 180°C/Gas 4. Dust the duck legs with flour and season with salt and pepper. Heat a heavy-based ovenproof sauté pan (or flameproof casserole) over a medium-high heat and add a good drizzle of olive oil. When hot, add the duck legs to the pan and colour for 4–5 minutes on each side. Remove and set aside.

Add the carrots, celeriac and onion to the pan, lower the heat and sweat for 4–5 minutes. Now add the bouquet garni and the orange zest and juice. Let bubble to reduce the juice down until the pan is almost dry. Pour in the red wine, bring to the boil and skim off any scum from the surface. Season with salt and pepper.

Return the duck legs to the pan, immersing them in the wine. Put a lid on the pan and cook in the oven for 1 hour or until the duck legs are tender but still holding their shape.

In the meantime, prepare the polenta. Bring the milk to the boil in a heavy-based saucepan. Season with salt, pepper and nutmeg and add the butter. Add the polenta in a steady stream, stirring as you do so, and cook, stirring frequently, for 15–20 minutes.

When the duck legs are cooked, remove them from the pan and set aside on a plate. Over a medium-high heat, let the braising liquor bubble rapidly to reduce by about half, then add the butter, chopped olives and basil. Discard the bouquet garni and orange zest.

Return the duck legs to the pan and spoon over the reduced liquor. Serve with the polenta.

RABBIT, CIDER & MUSTARD STEW.

I've found it difficult to persuade people to eat rabbit over the years, but once they've tried it most of them have really enjoyed it. To me, it's wonderfully tasty with a mild gamey flavour, more acceptable to most than hare or other game. Using cider as the braising liquor gives a lovely apple flavour to this dish.

Serves 4

2 rabbits, about 1.2kg each, jointed
plain flour for dusting
sea salt and freshly ground black
  pepper
olive oil for cooking
1 onion, peeled and chopped
½ leek, trimmed, washed and
  chopped
2 carrots, peeled and roughly chopped
2 celery sticks, de-strung and roughly
  chopped
½ garlic bulb (cut horizontally)
bouquet garni (see page 187)
1 litre cider
150ml chicken stock (see page 185),
  if needed
150ml double cream
10g butter
3–4 tablespoons grain mustard,
  to taste
1 tablespoon chopped chives

Heat the oven to 180°C/Gas 4. Dust the rabbit pieces with flour and season with salt and pepper. Heat a heavy-based ovenproof sauté pan (or flameproof casserole) over a medium heat and add a good drizzle of olive oil. Add the rabbit pieces and colour them all over for 6–8 minutes. Remove and set aside on a plate.

Add the onion, leek, carrots, celery and garlic to the pan with the bouquet garni. Lower the heat and sweat gently for 3–4 minutes to soften. Pour in the cider and bring to the boil. Replace the rabbit pieces in the pan, immersing them in the cider. Season with salt and pepper.

Put a lid on the pan and place in the oven. Cook for 1½–2 hours, checking occasionally and adding some chicken stock if the liquor appears be reducing down too much. Once cooked, remove the pieces of rabbit to a plate.

Over a medium-high heat, let the liquor bubble rapidly to reduce by half, then stir in the cream and bring to the boil. Whisk in the butter, stir in the mustard, then taste and adjust the seasoning.

Return the rabbit to the pan and spoon over the creamy mustard sauce. Sprinkle with chopped chives and serve with mashed potato or pasta.

You can use wild rabbit here, but I prefer the farmed option, which is better quality meat, if a little more expensive. The secret to a delicious rabbit stew is to dust the meat with flour and colour it first until lovely and golden.

VENISON STEW WITH CELERIAC & ORANGE.

I mostly cook venison in the autumn, but it can be stored in the freezer for several months to enjoy once the game season is over. I devised this dish recently when a friend came over for dinner and gave me a haunch of venison. It may be a Scottish thing, but I was over the moon! As with most game, root vegetables and fruit go well with venison. Use a good-quality red wine – not a premium one, but don't be tempted to buy a cheap bottle. **Serves 4**

1kg haunch of venison, cut into
  2–3cm pieces
plain flour for dusting
sea salt and freshly ground black
  pepper
olive oil for cooking
25g butter
50g bacon lardons
1 onion, peeled and chopped
1 celeriac, peeled and diced
3 carrots, peeled and diced
2 garlic cloves, peeled and roughly
  chopped
8 juniper berries
bouquet garni (see page 187)
finely pared zest of 1 orange
juice of 3 oranges
75cl bottle of full-bodied red wine
250ml chicken stock (see page 185),
  or more if needed
1 tablespoon chopped parsley

Heat the oven to 160°C/Gas 2–3. Dust the venison lightly with flour and season with salt and pepper. Heat a heavy-based ovenproof sauté pan (or flameproof casserole) over a medium heat and add a good drizzle of olive oil. You will need to brown the venison in two batches. When the oil is hot, add half of the venison pieces with half of the butter. Colour the meat all over for 4–5 minutes, then remove with a slotted spoon and set aside. Repeat with the second batch.

Return the pan to the heat and drizzle in a little more olive oil. Add the bacon lardons, onion, celeriac, carrots, garlic and juniper berries. Lower the heat slightly and sweat gently for 4–5 minutes, stirring occasionally. Add the bouquet garni and orange zest and sweat for another 2–3 minutes. Pour in the orange juice and let bubble to reduce by half.

Return the meat to the pan and pour in the red wine to cover. Bring to the boil and skim off any scum from the surface. Pour in the chicken stock and bring to a simmer. Season with salt and pepper, put a lid on the pan and place in the oven. Cook for 1½ hours or until the venison is tender, checking occasionally and topping up with a little more stock if needed.

Scatter the chopped parsley over the stew just before serving.

POT AU FEU.

This classic French country-style dish is one of my favourites. It's also versatile, as you can vary the meats and vegetables – I've included a ham hock here, which isn't traditional but it works well with the other flavours. To fully appreciate the meal, mustard and gherkins are a must. **Serves 4–6**

1 ham hock
1 smoked sausage, about 250g
200g piece of pancetta
500g piece of beef flank
1 garlic bulb, halved horizontally
6 black peppercorns
bouquet garni (see page 187)
sea salt and freshly ground black
  pepper
1 onion, peeled and quartered
2 carrots, peeled and halved
  lengthways
½ celeriac, peeled and cut into 4 pieces
2 turnips, peeled and halved
2 leeks, trimmed, washed and halved
  lengthways
1 Savoy cabbage, cut into quarters
thyme sprigs to garnish

To serve
English mustard
gherkins

Put the ham hock, smoked sausage, pancetta and beef flank into a cooking pot and pour on enough cold water to cover. Slowly bring to the boil and skim off any scum from the surface; this is the only time the stock should come to the boil.

Add the garlic, peppercorns, bouquet garni and a pinch of salt to the pot. Lower the heat and cook gently for 3½ hours; the stock should be below simmering, with just the occasional bubble breaking the surface.

Check the pieces of meat at this stage by insert a roasting fork into the thickest part; if the meat yields easily, it is nearly cooked, which is as it should be; if not cook, for a little longer.

Now add the onion, carrots, celeriac, turnips, leeks and cabbage wedges to the stock and cook gently for a further 30 minutes. Use a small knife to check each vegetable to ensure it is cooked.

When ready to serve, divide the meat into portions and place in warm serving bowls. Add a portion of vegetables to each bowl and a ladleful of the stock. Grind over some pepper, garnish with thyme sprigs and serve with mustard and gherkins.

BEEF & GUINNESS PIE.

Beef and Guinness are a classic combination for a stew, but feel free to experiment here with different local ales – I've come across some that work brilliantly. You can, of course, serve the filling without the pastry as a stew, perhaps adding some lightly browned, diced ox kidney. I often make double the quantity of stew and freeze half for another meal. **Serves 4**

1kg stewing steak, cut into 2–3cm pieces
flour for dusting
sea salt and freshly ground black pepper
olive oil for cooking
1 onion, peeled and diced
2 carrots, peeled and chopped
250g button mushrooms, cleaned
2 garlic cloves, peeled and chopped
bouquet garni (see page 187)
250ml red wine
500ml can Guinness or stout
250g ready-rolled puff pastry
eggwash (1 egg yolk, beaten with ½ teaspoon water and a pinch of salt)

Heat the oven to 150°C/Gas 2. Dust the pieces of stewing steak all over with flour and season with salt and pepper. Heat a heavy-based ovenproof sauté pan over a medium-high heat and add a good drizzle of olive oil. Brown the beef in two batches for 4–5 minutes until well caramelised. Remove with a slotted spoon and set aside.

Return the pan to the heat and add another drizzle of oil. Add the onion, carrots and mushrooms, lower the heat and sweat gently for 4–5 minutes. Add the garlic and bouquet garni.

Pour in the red wine and let bubble to reduce by half, then add the Guinness or stout. Bring back to the boil and then return the beef to the pan. Put a lid on the pan and place in the oven. Cook for 3 hours or until the beef is tender and the liquor has reduced and thickened.

Raise the oven setting to 180°C/Gas 4. Transfer the beef stew to a pie dish, discarding the bouquet garni. Cut out a disc of pastry large enough to cover the pie dish generously (allow about 3cm extra all round). Dampen the rim of the dish with water, then lift the pastry over the top of the stew. Press the edges of the pastry onto the rim of the dish and trim away the excess pastry.

Brush the pastry lid with eggwash and bake the pie in the oven for 15–20 minutes until the pastry is golden brown and crisp. Serve with seasonal vegetables.

BRAISED LAMB SHANKS WITH CUMIN & FLAGEOLET BEANS.

Lamb shanks are one of the most popular of the less expensive, flavourful cuts of lamb. With long, slow cooking, they become meltingly tender. Here I'm braising them with flageolet beans and tomatoes for a lovely comfort dish. If you're planning ahead, rather than using tinned beans, soak 200g dried flageolets in cold water to cover overnight, then cook in water to cover for an hour before draining and adding to the pan with the tomatoes. **Serves 4**

4 lamb shanks
sea salt and freshly ground black
 pepper
olive oil for cooking
1 onion, peeled and sliced
2 fennel bulbs, trimmed and sliced
2 garlic cloves, peeled and chopped
1 teaspoon fennel seeds
1 tablespoon ground cumin
bouquet garni (see page 187)
2 tablespoons tomato purée
300ml white wine
500g chopped tomatoes (full-
 flavoured fresh or tinned)
500ml lamb stock (see page 186)
 or chicken stock (see page 185)
400g tin flageolet beans, drained
 (or cooked dried beans, see above)
1 tablespoon chopped parsley

Heat the oven to 160°C/Gas 2–3. Season the lamb shanks well all over with salt and pepper. Heat a deep heavy-based ovenproof sauté pan (or flameproof casserole) over a medium-high heat and add a drizzle of olive oil. Brown the lamb shanks in the pan (in two batches, or one at a time if that's easier) to colour all over. Place the browned shanks on a plate on the side.

Return the pan to a medium-low heat and add a little more oil if needed, followed by the onion, sliced fennel, garlic, fennel seeds and ground cumin. Add the bouquet garni and sweat gently for 3–4 minutes. Stir in the tomato purée and cook for a further 2 minutes.

Pour in the white wine and let bubble to reduce by half. Add the tomatoes and stock and bring to the boil, then stir in the flageolet beans. Replace the lamb shanks in the pan, immersing them in the tomato mixture.

Put a lid on the pan and place in the oven. Cook for 1½ hours until the meat is very soft and starting to fall from the bone.

Place a lamb shank in each warm serving bowl and spoon on the tomato and flageolet bean mixture. Sprinkle with chopped parsley to serve.

DAUBE OF PORK CHEEKS.

This is an adaptation of the classic French *daube de boeuf* and you need to start preparing it a day ahead to allow plenty of time for the meat to marinate. Don't be alarmed by the amount of red wine required… The end result – a wonderfully rich red wine sauce to complement the pork cheeks – is well worth it. It's an ideal dish for a winter dinner party. If you can't get hold of pork cheeks, you can use ox cheeks or even a jointed chicken instead. **Serves 4**

16 pork cheeks, trimmed of fat
   and sinew

Marinade
75cl bottle of red wine
2 carrots, peeled and chopped
1 onion, peeled and chopped
1 bouquet garni (see page 187)
½ garlic bulb, cut horizontally
1 teaspoon black peppercorns

Daube
plain flour for dusting
sea salt and freshly ground black
   pepper
olive oil for cooking
2 carrots, peeled and chopped
1 onion, peeled and chopped
1 bouquet garni (see page 187)
½ garlic bulb, cut horizontally
1 teaspoon black peppercorns
100g small chestnut or button
   mushrooms, cleaned
75cl bottle of red wine
25g butter
1 tablespoon chopped parsley
   (optional)

A day ahead, put the pork cheeks into a colander and rinse under cold running water for 5 minutes or so, to clean thoroughly. Drain the pork cheeks and pat dry with kitchen paper. Put them into a clean bowl and pour on enough red wine to cover (keep the rest for the daube). Add the carrots, onion, bouquet garni, garlic and black peppercorns. Cover and place in the fridge to marinate for 24 hours.

The following day, remove the pork cheeks from the wine and pat dry on kitchen paper; discard the marinade. Heat the oven to 150°C/Gas 2.

Lightly dust the marinated pork cheeks with flour and season with salt and pepper. Heat a heavy-based ovenproof sauté pan (or flameproof casserole) over a medium-high heat and add a good drizzle of olive oil. Now add the pork cheeks to the pan and colour all over for 4–5 minutes. Remove the cheeks from the pan and set aside on a plate.

Return the pan to the heat and add another drizzle of olive oil. Add the carrots, onion, bouquet garni, garlic, black peppercorns and mushrooms. Lower the heat slightly and sweat gently for 3–4 minutes.

Now place the pig cheeks on top of the vegetables and pour on enough red wine to cover. Bring to the boil and skim off any scum from the surface. Season with salt and pepper.

Put a lid on the pan and place in the oven. Cook for 1½–2 hours until the cheeks are soft and tender, checking occasionally and adding more wine to cover the cheeks if necessary. Once cooked, remove the pork cheeks to a plate.

Over a medium-high heat, let the liquor bubble to reduce by half to make a rich red wine sauce. Stir in the butter to give it a shine, then taste and adjust the seasoning.

To serve, place 4 pork cheeks in each warm serving bowl with the vegetables. Pour on the red wine sauce and sprinkle with chopped parsley if you wish. Serve with tagliatelle and glazed carrots.

PORK BELLY BRAISED WITH STAR ANISE & FENNEL SEEDS.

This is a great dish to prepare in advance and serve up for a casual evening with friends. Pork belly is something people often love, but it can be disappointing if it's not cooked correctly. You'll need to start preparing this dish a day or two ahead, as the pork needs to be braised, pressed and chilled, but it's well worth the wait – not least because the stock provides the basis for another meal (see below). **Serves 4**

1kg piece of pork belly
sea salt and freshly ground black
* pepper*
olive oil for cooking
4 chunky carrots, peeled and roughly
* chopped*
1 white onion, peeled and quartered
1 fennel bulb, trimmed and quartered
4 star anise
1 teaspoon fennel seeds
½ garlic bulb (cut horizontally)
bouquet garni (see page 187)
500ml chicken stock (see page 185)

Heat the oven to 180°C/Gas 4. Season the pork belly all over with salt and pepper. Heat a heavy-based ovenproof cooking pot over a medium-high heat and add a little olive oil. Place the pork belly, skin side down, in the pot and sear for 3–4 minutes to brown, then turn and colour the other side for 3–4 minutes. Remove from the pan and set aside.

Add the carrots, onion and fennel to the pot and cook over a medium-low heat for 5 minutes. Add the star anise, fennel seeds, garlic and bouquet garni and sweat for a further 3–4 minutes.

Lay the pork belly on the vegetables, pour on the chicken stock, season with salt and bring to the boil. Put the lid on and transfer the pot to the oven. Cook for 2–2½ hours until the pork is tender.

Carefully lift the pork out of the pot and allow to cool. Drain the vegetables, reserving them and the liquor. Line a baking tray with cling film, place the pork on the tray and wrap in the cling film. Cover with another tray, then place a weight on top (a heavy chopping board is ideal). Place in the fridge and leave to compress for 24 hours. Refrigerate the vegetables and liquor too.

The next day, when ready to serve, heat the oven to 170°C/Gas 3. Unwrap the pork. Heat a non-stick ovenproof frying pan over a medium-high heat. Add a drizzle of olive oil and place the pork, skin side down, in the pan – take care, as the fat will spit. Fry for 4–5 minutes, then transfer to the oven. Cook for 12–15 minutes until crispy, turning the pork once or twice. Remove the fat from the reserved liquor. Reheat the vegetables in some of the liquor.

Slice the pork belly and serve with the vegetables, spooning a little of the hot liquor over them.

The braising liquor is infused with wonderful, complex flavours during the long, slow cooking, making it an excellent base for a tasty soup. For a pork, noodle and ginger broth, simply cook the noodles in the stock and add some shredded fresh ginger and chopped vegetables, along with a good handful of pork trimmings.

BREADS & SAVOURY NIBBLES

FOCACCIA WITH ROSEMARY.

Focaccia epitomises everything I love about Mediterranean food – its simplicity and wonderful, rustic flavours. I especially enjoy eating this classic Italian flat bread with cured meats, a leafy salad and a tomato and basil salad dressed with good olive oil. It's fun to make and you can vary the topping – try chopped olives and sun-dried tomatoes in place of rosemary and sea salt, for example. **Serves 4**

375ml lukewarm water
1 sachet active dried yeast (7g)
500g strong white bread flour
2 teaspoons salt
4 tablespoons finely chopped rosemary
5 tablespoons extra virgin olive oil
sea salt flakes for sprinkling

Pour 100ml of the warm water into a jug, sprinkle on the dried yeast, stir and set aside for 10 minutes. Meanwhile, in a large bowl (preferably of an electric mixer, fitted with a dough hook), combine the flour, salt and half of the chopped rosemary.

Mix the yeast liquid with the remaining 275ml warm water and 2 tablespoons of the extra virgin olive oil. Using an electric mixer, or by hand, work the liquid ingredients into the flour mixture to form a smooth, soft dough. Transfer to a lightly oiled bowl, cover the dough with lightly oiled cling film and leave to rise in a warm place for about 1–1½ hours until doubled in size.

Knock back the dough in the bowl, then turn out onto a lightly floured surface. Shape roughly into a 25cm circle, flattening the dough gently with floured hands.

Line a baking tray with baking parchment, oil lightly and sprinkle with flour. Carefully transfer the dough to the baking tray and cover with oiled cling film. Leave to prove until nearly doubled in size; this will take about 45 minutes. Meanwhile, heat the oven to 200°C/Gas 6.

Once the dough is ready, mix the remaining olive oil with 1 tablespoon water. Make indentations over the surface of the dough with your fingertips (see below). Brush the dough with the oil and water mixture, then scatter over the remaining chopped rosemary and sprinkle generously with sea salt flakes.

Bake the focaccia for 20–25 minutes until well risen and golden. Transfer to a wire rack to cool slightly. Serve warm.

To give focaccia its characteristic dimpled surface, you need to make holes all over the surface of the dough before baking. As it's a very sticky dough to handle, flour your fingertips before poking them into the dough to make the indentations.

CRISPY PASTA BREAD.

This is a great party snack to have with an apéritif. I often serve it with crudités and a blue cheese dressing (see page 43). You can vary the topping, sprinkling the dough with caraway seeds, poppy seeds or even chilli oil to give a variety of flavourings. To enjoy it at its crispest, eat this bread on the day it is made, but if you have some left over, store it in an airtight container to eat the following day. **Serves 4–6**

180ml lukewarm water
3 sachets active dried yeast (20g)
400g plain flour
40g butter, melted
20ml olive oil, plus extra for brushing
1 teaspoon chopped rosemary
sea salt

Pour the warm water into a jug, stir in the yeast and set aside for 10 minutes. Put the flour into a bowl. Stir the butter and olive oil into the yeast mix, then add to the flour and mix to a smooth dough. Cover with a damp cloth and leave to rise in a warm place for 30 minutes. Meanwhile, heat the oven to 240°C/Gas 9.

Knock back the dough and cut into four equal pieces. Roll out one piece, using a pasta machine if you have one, or on a lightly floured surface with a rolling pin until paper-thin. Line a baking tray with baking parchment and carefully lift the dough on top.

Brush the dough with olive oil and sprinkle with rosemary and sea salt. Bake in the very hot oven for 3–4 minutes until golden. Repeat with the rest of the dough. Cool on a wire rack.

PANISSE.

These chickpea flour chips (illustrated on page 2) are a speciality of Nice in the south of France, where *socca* (chickpea pancakes) are also popular. Serve as a tasty alternative to potato chips, with meat or fish, or with a rustic salad. **Serves 4**

200ml water
sea salt and freshly ground black
  pepper
2 tablespoons olive oil
100g chickpea flour
oil for deep-frying

Bring the water to the boil in a heavy-based saucepan and add a good pinch of salt and all but 1 teaspoon of the olive oil. When the water is boiling, whisk in the flour and cook gently, stirring frequently, for 12–15 minutes. Transfer the mixture to a blender and work until smooth, adding the remaining olive oil.

Line a tray with baking parchment and spread the mixture out on the paper, flattening it roughly to a 3cm depth. Place in the fridge to firm up for 6 hours.

Heat the oil in a deep-fryer or deep, heavy pan to 160°C. Cut the dough into thick chips and deep-fry in batches as necessary for 3–4 minutes until golden and crisp. Remove and drain on kitchen paper. Season well with salt and pepper and serve.

COTTAGE CHEESE & DILL BREAD.

This recipe works so well because there is a lovely balance between the cheese and yeast dough, with the dill adding a fresh touch. I must thank Mandy, my impressive American pastry chef at The Kitchin, for sharing the recipe with me; it's one that her mother has made for decades. I often make a couple of loaves when we are having a barbecue at home – they always go down a treat. **Makes 2 loaves**

120ml lukewarm water
2 sachets dried yeast (14g)
540g strong white bread flour
2 teaspoons salt
1 teaspoon baking powder
2 tablespoons very finely diced onion
480g cottage cheese
2 tablespoons sugar
2 tablespoons dill leaves, very finely
    chopped
2 free-range medium eggs, lightly
    beaten
1 teaspoon coarse sea salt for
    sprinkling

Pour the warm water into a jug, sprinkle on the dried yeast, stir and set aside for 10 minutes until the yeast has fully dissolved.

Grease and flour two 500g loaf tins. Sift the flour, salt and baking powder into a large bowl and make a well in the centre.

In another bowl, combine the onion, cottage cheese, sugar, chopped dill and beaten eggs, then stir in the yeast mixture. Slowly pour this mixture into the flour and mix with your hands to form a stiff dough.

Turn the dough out onto a lightly floured surface and knead until smooth and elastic. Now place the dough in a large oiled bowl and cover with lightly oiled cling film. Leave to rise in a warm place for about an hour until doubled in size.

Knock back the dough, knead lightly and divide in half. Pat each portion of dough out into an oblong, about 25 x 15cm. Then roll each one into a tightish coil, tucking the ends underneath so it will just fit into the loaf tin.

Put the dough into the loaf tins and cover lightly with a cloth or lightly oiled cling film. Leave to prove until the dough almost reaches the top of the tins; this should take about 40 minutes. Meanwhile, heat the oven to 190°C/Gas 5.

Bake the loaves for 35–45 minutes until they are deep golden brown on top and sound hollow when tapped on the bottom.

Sprinkle the coarse sea salt on top of the loaves. Leave in the tins for 5 minutes, then transfer to a wire rack to cool. Serve while still slightly warm.

MUSHROOM BRIOCHES.

The idea for this savoury brioche came from one of the legendary chefs I once worked for in Paris, Guy Savoy. I love its earthy mushroom flavour, especially with pâté or alongside a soup. Served slightly warm or toasted, it is just heavenly. **Makes 10–12 mini brioches**

180ml lukewarm milk
1½ sachets active dried yeast (10g)
4 free-range medium eggs
560g plain flour
15g salt
50g sugar
340g unsalted butter, softened

Mushroom duxelle

400g button mushrooms, cleaned
20g butter
1 tablespoon finely chopped shallot
2 garlic cloves, peeled and finely chopped
1 teaspoon dried herbes de Provence
sea salt and freshly ground black pepper

Eggwash

2 egg yolks beaten with 1 teaspoon water and a pinch of salt

Pour the milk into a jug, sprinkle on the dried yeast and leave for 10–15 minutes, until the yeast is fully dissolved and the liquid begins to froth. Add the eggs to the yeast liquid, beating lightly to break them down.

Combine the flour, salt and sugar in the bowl of an electric mixer fitted with a dough hook and mix briefly. Now, with the motor running, slowly pour in the yeast, milk and egg mix. Continue to work on a medium speed for 5–7 minutes.

Once the dough appears smooth and elastic, begin adding the butter, little by little, until it is all incorporated. Continue mixing for a further 5 minutes. When ready, the dough should appear very smooth and shiny.

Turn the dough out into a lightly oiled large bowl. Cover with lightly oiled cling film and leave to rise in a warm place until doubled in size; this should take about an hour.

In the meantime, prepare the mushroom duxelle. Chop the mushrooms into small dice. Heat a heavy-based pan over a medium-low heat. Add the butter and, once melted and foaming, add the mushrooms, shallot, garlic, dried herbs and some seasoning. Cook for 3–4 minutes to soften and release all the liquid from the mushrooms. Then increase the heat to drive off the liquid; the pan should be quite dry. Set aside to cool.

Lightly grease and flour 10–12 metal rings, 7.5cm in diameter, and stand on a baking sheet. Turn the risen dough onto a floured surface and knead lightly. Divide the dough in half. Roll each half into a rectangle, about 40 x 20cm and 1cm thick. Spread the mushroom duxelle on top of the two sheets of dough, leaving a 1cm margin along the edges.

Starting at a long edge, roll each rectangle of dough up like a Swiss roll, finishing with the seam underneath. Cut into 7.5cm lengths and place in the prepared rings. Cover with lightly oiled cling film and allow to prove until they have almost reached the top of the rings. Meanwhile, heat the oven to 180°C/Gas 4.

Brush the brioches with eggwash and bake for 15 minutes until deep golden. Leave in the tins for 5 minutes, then turn out onto a wire rack to cool. Serve while still slightly warm.

DRIED FRUIT & WALNUT BREAD.

This richly fruited, soft-textured bread is outstanding with cheese and it has featured on the cheese trolley in the restaurant over the years. The recipe, which was given to me by a German friend, is quite easy, but as the dough is very moist, you really need to use an electric mixer. The bread freezes well, so I always make several loaves and freeze what I don't need to enjoy another day. **Makes 3 loaves**

100ml lukewarm water
1½ sachets active dried yeast (10g)
100g plain flour
1kg prunes, pitted
250g sultanas
100g dried apricots, roughly chopped
100g dried cranberries
150g walnuts, roughly chopped

In a bowl, mix the water, dried yeast and 75g of the flour together to form a smooth batter. Cover and leave in a warm place for about 30 minutes, or until well risen and full of air bubbles.

Transfer the yeast batter to an electric mixer fitted with a dough hook and add the rest of the flour, the dried fruit and walnuts. Mix on a low speed for 7–10 minutes until the prunes begin to break down, forming a sticky, brown dough.

Turn the dough out onto a floured surface and divide into three equal portions. Using plenty of flour, roll each portion into a log, about 20cm long. Place on an oiled baking tray, cover and leave to stand at room temperature for an hour. Meanwhile, heat the oven to 170°C/Gas 3.

Bake the loaves for 20–25 minutes until rich brown and slightly crusty on the outside; they will still feel soft in the middle. Allow the loaves to cool, then wrap each one in cling film and chill in the fridge to firm up.

Once chilled, the bread can be sliced very thinly and served with cheese.

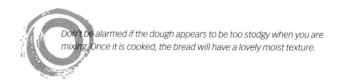

Don't be alarmed if the dough appears to be too stodgy when you are mixing. Once it is cooked, the bread will have a lovely moist texture.

GOUGÈRES.

When we have friends over I often serve these with pre-dinner drinks, along with cheese straws. I like to use a local Cheddar – we are fortunate to have several to choose from. **Makes about 25**

250ml water
15g sea salt
125g unsalted butter
250g plain flour
6 free-range medium eggs, beaten
4 tablespoons grated full-flavoured
    Cheddar
flaky sea salt and cracked black pepper

Heat the oven to 200°C/Gas 6. Bring the water to the boil in a saucepan. Add the salt and butter and continue to heat until the butter melts and the liquid comes to the boil. Immediately tip in the flour and mix quickly with a wooden spoon until the paste thickens and leaves the sides of the pan.

Remove from the heat and let cool a little for about 5 minutes. Now gradually beat in the eggs and incorporate the cheese. The mixture should be smooth and thick enough to pipe.

Line a baking tray with baking parchment. Put the choux pastry into a piping fitted with a 1cm plain nozzle and pipe small balls onto the tray, spacing them slightly apart. Bake for 20 minutes until dry and crisp on the outside but still soft inside.

Serve the little gougères warm from the oven, sprinkled with flaky sea salt and cracked pepper.

CHEDDAR CHEESE STRAWS WITH CARAWAY.

A tasty, easy-to-prepare snack to enjoy with an apéritif. The dough freezes brilliantly, so I always roll it out in smaller sheets and freeze some to have on hand for unexpected visitors. The base defrosts in no time, ready to cut into straws, bake and serve warm from the oven. **Makes about 25**

400g plain flour
20g sea salt
500g full-flavoured Cheddar, grated
10g caraway seeds
30g English mustard
225g butter, melted

Mix the flour, salt, cheese and caraway seeds together in a bowl until evenly combined. Add the mustard and butter and mix to bind together to a smooth, firm dough. Wrap in cling film and chill for 30 minutes.

Heat the oven to 180°C/Gas 4. Unwrap the pastry and roll out in two or three batches to a 1cm thickness. (At this stage, wrap and chill or freeze any dough you are not serving straight away.)

Cut the dough into strips, about 10cm long and 1cm wide, and place slightly apart on a baking sheet. Bake for 5 minutes until golden brown.

Carefully transfer the cheese straws to a wire rack to cool slightly before serving.

PRETZELS.

Originally a German recipe, pretzels have been replicated all over the world and now come in sweet, savoury and salty variations – with or without nuts, seeds or sea salt. There are numerous options and it's easy to create your own bespoke pretzels. I usually keep mine plain, but slightly salted, to eat with a cream cheese and chive dip, or a honey and mustard dressing. **Makes 8–10**

240ml lukewarm water
1 sachet active dried yeast (7g)
350g plain flour
½ teaspoon salt
1 tablespoon sugar
30g butter, softened

To poach
2 litres water
50g bicarbonate of soda

To finish
eggwash (2 eggs yolks, beaten with
 1 teaspoon water and a pinch of salt)
coarse sea salt and/or poppy, sesame
 or pumpkin seeds for sprinkling

Pour the warm water into a jug, sprinkle on the dried yeast, stir and set aside for 10 minutes until the yeast is fully dissolved.

Put the flour, salt and sugar into the bowl of an electric mixer fitted with a dough hook. Work in the butter, followed by the yeast liquid. Continue to work the dough until it is smooth and no longer sticky.

Transfer to a lightly oiled bowl, cover the dough with lightly oiled cling film and leave to rise in a warm place for about 45 minutes to an hour until doubled in size.

Lightly grease two large baking trays. Knock back the dough, knead lightly and divide into 8–10 equal pieces. Using as little flour as possible, roll the dough into long sausage shapes, about 50cm long and 1.5cm thick.

Form each sausage into a pretzel shape, folding one end over the other and sticking the ends down using a little egg wash. Place on the prepared baking tray and cover with lightly oiled cling film. Leave the pretzels to prove for 35–40 minutes until slightly less than doubled in size.

Heat the oven to 180°C/Gas 4. To poach the pretzels, pour the water into a large (non-aluminium) cooking pot, add the bicarbonate of soda and bring to the boil. You will need to poach the pretzels a few at a time. Carefully lower them, one by one, into the boiling water and poach for about 1 minute, until they float to the surface. Remove with a slotted spoon and drain briefly on kitchen paper before placing back on the baking sheets. Repeat with the rest of the pretzels.

Brush the pretzels with egg wash and sprinkle liberally with coarse salt and/or seeds. Bake for 10–12 minutes until deep brown and crisp on the outside. Transfer to a wire rack to cool. Serve while still warm.

EASY STARTERS

ASPARAGUS SOUP TOPPED WITH RICOTTA, CHIVES & CRISPY CHICKEN.

I treasure asparagus during its short six-week season in late spring/early summer as it's the only time I eat it; the flavour of imported asparagus is so inferior by comparison. If you have an asparagus farm nearby you may be able to buy 'soup asparagus', which is cheaper because the spears aren't perfectly shaped, but are just as flavourful. You can serve the soup hot or cold. Shaved raw asparagus and crispy chicken with ricotta and chives give a lovely contrasting finish. **Serves 4**

800g asparagus spears
olive oil for cooking
1 white onion, peeled and sliced
sea salt and freshly ground black
  pepper
450ml chicken stock (see page 185)
50g baby spinach leaves

Chicken and ricotta garnish
12 chicken wings
olive oil for cooking
1 teaspoon caraway seeds
150g ricotta
1 teaspoon chopped chives

To finish
4 asparagus spears, trimmed
extra virgin olive oil
freshly cracked black pepper

To prepare the asparagus for the soup, snap off the woody ends of the spears and peel the lower end of the stalks. Finely chop the asparagus. Heat a heavy-based saucepan over a medium heat and add a drizzle of olive oil. Add the onion, season with a little salt and sweat gently for 2–3 minutes to soften. Meanwhile, bring the chicken stock to the boil in another pan.

Add the asparagus to the onion and sweat together over a high heat for 1–2 minutes. Pour in enough of the hot stock to just cover the asparagus. Simmer for 5–6 minutes until the asparagus is just cooked, adding a little more stock to keep it covered if needed. Add the spinach and cook very briefly until it just wilts.

Tip the soup into a blender and blitz until smooth. Taste and adjust the seasoning. Unless serving hot straight away, transfer to a bowl and cool quickly over another bowl of ice to preserve the lovely vivid green colour, then cover and refrigerate.

Heat the oven to 180°C/Gas 4. For the garnish, put the chicken wings into a bowl, drizzle with olive oil and toss to coat. Sprinkle with salt, pepper and the caraway seeds. Heat a large non-stick ovenproof frying pan over a medium-high heat and add a drizzle of olive oil. Add the chicken wings and colour for 3–4 minutes on each side. Transfer the pan to the oven for 8–10 minutes until the wings are cooked through. Set aside to cool slightly.

Once cooled, pull the meat from the bone. Tear into strips and put into a bowl with the ricotta and chives. Mix together and season with salt and pepper to taste.

When ready to serve, trim the 4 raw asparagus spears (as above), then cut lengthways into fine slices, using a sharp knife. Rub with extra virgin olive oil and season with salt and pepper. If serving the soup hot, reheat it gently.

Divide the soup between bowls and top each portion with a generous spoonful of the ricotta mixture and the raw asparagus slices. Top the ricotta with a sprinkling of cracked pepper and drizzle a little extra virgin olive oil around the soup.

MUSSELS IN A CREAMY CIDER BROTH WITH LEEK, POTATO & APPLE.

I adore mussels and *moules frites* happens to be one of my all-time favourite suppers. For this beautiful starter, the mussels are steamed open in cider rather than the usual white wine and served in a creamy broth made from the cooking liquor. It's worth spending a bit more for a good-quality cider here. **Serves 4**

1.5kg mussels in shell
2 potatoes, peeled and diced
sea salt and freshly ground black
   pepper
½ leek, trimmed, washed and diced
olive oil for cooking
3 shallots, peeled and sliced
1 tablespoon shredded parsley
300ml good-quality cider
100ml double cream
50g butter, in pieces
2 green-skinned dessert apples
100ml crème fraîche
1 tablespoon chopped chives

Clean the mussels thoroughly (see below). Add the diced potatoes to a pan of boiling salted water and cook until just tender; remove and set aside. Repeat with the chopped leek.

Meanwhile, heat a large heavy-based saucepan over a high heat and add a good drizzle of olive oil. Add the shallots and cook, stirring, for about 30 seconds. Now add the mussels and parsley, pour in the cider and immediately put a tight-fitting lid on the pan. Steam for about 2 minutes until the mussels are all open, shaking the pan occasionally. Drain in a colander over a bowl to catch the liquor. Discard any mussels that have not opened.

Return the liquor to the pan and let bubble to reduce by a third. Stir in the cream and butter and cook, stirring occasionally, for 2–3 minutes to reduce and thicken slightly.

In the meantime, remove most of the mussels from their shells, leaving eight in their shells for the garnish. Halve, core and dice the apples.

Stir the crème fraîche into the creamy broth and heat through, stirring. Season with salt and pepper to taste. Now, using a handheld stick blender, blitz the liquor until frothy.

Divide the shelled mussels, diced potatoes, leek and apples between warm bowls and pour in the hot creamy broth. Serve at once, garnished with the reserved mussels and scattered with the chopped chives.

To clean mussels, scrub the shells under cold running water and pull away the hairy 'beard' from the side of each shell. Discard any with cracked or damaged shells. Gently tap any open mussels with the back of a knife and check that they close; if not they are dead and must be discarded.

LEEKS WITH SAUCE GRIBICHE.

When in season, young leeks are full of flavour and cook until meltingly tender. Here I'm baking them in a foil parcel to seal in all the flavours. It is important to check that the leeks are tender right through; if they are undercooked the dish won't taste the same. The acidity of the gherkins and capers in the sauce offsets the sweetness of the leeks perfectly. **Serves 4**

4 young leeks
olive oil to drizzle
sea salt and freshly ground black
*   pepper*
1 bunch of thyme
4 garlic cloves (unpeeled)
50g butter, in pieces

Sauce gribiche
4 free-range medium eggs
1 teaspoon Dijon mustard
25ml white wine vinegar
250ml vegetable oil
30g capers, drained, rinsed and
*   chopped*
30g gherkins, chopped
1 tablespoon chopped parsley

Heat the oven to 160°C/Gas 2–3. Remove the outer leaves from the leeks and trim the root end, being careful to keep it intact as this will hold the leek together during cooking. Make two lengthways cuts through the top third of each leek to access any grit, then wash the leeks thoroughly. Drain and pat dry with kitchen paper.

Lay a large sheet of strong foil in a roasting tin. Place the leeks side by side on the foil, drizzle with olive oil and season with salt and pepper. Scatter over the thyme sprigs and garlic cloves, and dot with the butter.

Lay another sheet of foil on top and then fold the edges of the two pieces of foil together to create a sealed parcel. Bake for 1 hour or until the leeks are tender.

Meanwhile, for the sauce, lower the eggs into a pan of boiling water and simmer for 8–9 minutes. Drain. Cool under running cold water, then peel and finely dice the eggs; set aside. In a separate bowl, whisk the mustard and wine vinegar together, then slowly add the oil, whisking to emulsify the sauce. Fold in the chopped capers, gherkins and parsley, then the diced hard-boiled eggs.

Serve the baked leeks with the sauce gribiche.

GOAT'S CHEESE WRAPPED IN PARMA HAM WITH MARINATED RED PEPPERS & BASIL.

A dish I enjoyed many years ago in Portofino on the Italian Riviera, while I was working on a private yacht, gave me the idea for this starter. Over the years, I've varied the flavourings, but the core ingredients – cheese, ham, peppers and basil – have remained the same. I think of it as Mediterranean cooking with a British touch. **Serves 4**

olive oil for cooking
3 red peppers
sea salt and freshly ground black pepper
4 pickled garlic cloves, sliced
1 tablespoon chopped black olives
1 tablespoon sherry vinegar
2 small goat's cheeses
4 large slices of Parma ham
large handful of basil leaves, shredded
handful of rocket leaves

Heat the oven to 180°C/Gas 4. Heat a non-stick ovenproof frying pan and add a drizzle of olive oil. Add the whole peppers, season with salt and pepper and sauté for 1–2 minutes. Transfer the pan to the oven and roast the peppers for 12–15 minutes until soft. On removing from the oven, place the peppers in a bowl and cover tightly with cling film. Set aside for 10 minutes; the steam created will help to lift the skins.

Remove the peppers from the bowl, peel off the skins, then cut them in half and remove the seeds and membranes. Slice the red peppers into strips and place in a bowl. Add a drizzle of olive oil, the pickled garlic slices, chopped olives, sherry vinegar and some seasoning. Toss to combine and set aside.

Cut each goat's cheese in half and loosely wrap a slice of Parma ham around each half (see below). Place the parcels on a baking tray in the oven for 4–5 minutes until the cheese starts to melt.

Meanwhile, add the shredded basil to the red pepper mixture and toss to combine. Spoon onto a platter or individual plates. Top with the goat's cheese parcels and scatter over a few rocket leaves to serve. Accompany with warm, crusty bread.

Lay the slices of Parma ham on your work surface, with a short side towards you. Place a halved goat's cheese on the end closest to you and loosely roll the ham around the cheese to enclose it.

CURRIED CRAYFISH COCKTAIL ON RYE BREAD.

Inspired by Scandinavian dishes I have enjoyed on my trips to Sweden, this is my twist on the ubiquitous prawn cocktail. It's a fun, fresh, colourful, easy starter and you can prepare the elements ahead, ready to assemble just before you sit down to eat. The curry kick in the dressing really brings the crayfish to life.
Serves 4

100ml mayonnaise (see page 187)
1 teaspoon curry powder
1 tablespoon chopped dill, plus extra
    sprigs to garnish
2 spring onions, trimmed and sliced
sea salt and freshly ground black
    pepper
squeeze of lemon juice, to taste
250g cooked, peeled crayfish
2 baby gem lettuces
¼ cucumber
4–5 radishes
1 avocado
4 slices of rye bread

In a large bowl, mix the mayonnaise with the curry powder, chopped dill and spring onions until evenly combined, adding salt and pepper and a squeeze of lemon juice to taste. Add the crayfish to the dressing, toss to coat and set aside.

Next, prepare the salad. Separate the lettuce leaves. Slice the cucumber lengthways into fine julienne, avoiding the core and seeds in the middle. Slice the radishes. Halve the avocado, remove the stone and peel away the skin, then slice thinly.

Arrange the salad ingredients decoratively on the rye bread. Pile the crayfish in their dressing on top and scatter over some dill sprigs to garnish. Serve at once.

MACKEREL ESCABECHE.

Mackerel was the very first fish I caught as a youngster and it is now a staple on my summer menu – both at the restaurant and at home. Sustainable and healthy, it's also great value for money, but it must be eaten extremely fresh. Here I have added my own lively flavour twist to the traditional Mediterranean technique of escabeche, with orange and fennel seeds. **Serves 4**

4 line-caught mackerel fillets
50ml extra virgin olive oil
2 carrots, peeled and sliced
4 shallots, peeled and sliced
bouquet garni (see page 187)
3 star anise
1 teaspoon fennel seeds, crushed
1 teaspoon coriander seeds, crushed
200ml white wine
juice of 4 oranges
400ml fish stock (see page 185)
sea salt and freshly ground black
* pepper*

Check the mackerel fillets for pin-bones, removing any you find with kitchen tweezers.

Heat the extra virgin olive oil in a heavy-based wide pan, add the carrots and sweat over a medium heat for 4–5 minutes. Add the shallots, bouquet garni, star anise, fennel and coriander seeds and sweat for a further 2–3 minutes.

Pour in the white wine, orange juice and fish stock and cook slowly, uncovered, for 10–12 minutes until the carrots are just tender; check with a small, sharp knife.

Now place the mackerel fillets, skin side up, on top of the vegetables, making sure the fillets are covered by the liquid. Cook for 2 minutes and then remove the pan from the heat.

Cover the pan tightly with cling film and set aside for 5 minutes; the mackerel will continue to cook in the residual heat.

Remove the cling film. Taste for seasoning, adding salt and pepper as needed, then serve the escabeche.

SALMON TARTARE WITH APPLE, DRIED CRANBERRIES & CRÈME FRAÎCHE.

This dish works with most raw fish, as long as it's super-fresh. I am lucky to get my fish delivered daily by local fishermen, who land their catch just a few minutes away from the restaurant. Here I've used salmon, but I also enjoy this dish with sea bass, mackerel and scallops. The acidity of the apples and sweetness of the cranberries balance the richness of the salmon and give the dish a lovely contrast of textures. **Serves 4**

300g salmon fillet, skinned
2 tablespoons finely diced shallots
2 tablespoons chopped chives
juice of 1 lemon
2 tablespoons light soy sauce
2 tablespoons rice vinegar
extra virgin olive oil to drizzle
sea salt and freshly ground black
*   pepper*
1 Granny Smith or other crisp
*   green apple*
1 red apple
50g dried cranberries, chopped
100ml crème fraîche

If you have time, put your chopping board in the freezer for 20 minutes before you start preparing the salmon; this will help you achieve a fine dice. Check the salmon for pin-bones.

Using a very sharp knife, cut the salmon on the chilled board into small dice and place in a bowl. You can do this ahead and set the bowl over ice to keep the salmon chilled.

Just before serving, add 1 tablespoon shallots, 1 tablespoon chives, the juice of ½ lemon, the soy sauce and rice vinegar to the diced salmon. Add a drizzle of extra virgin olive oil and mix together, seasoning well with salt and pepper; set aside.

Quarter and core the apples, then cut into fine dice. Place in another bowl with the remaining shallots, chives and lemon juice, the dried cranberries and a drizzle of olive oil. Toss to mix, seasoning with salt to taste.

To serve, place the salmon on individual plates and top with the diced apple mixture. Finish with a spoonful of crème fraîche and a grinding of pepper.

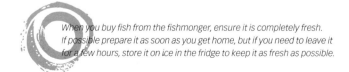

When you buy fish from the fishmonger, ensure it is completely fresh. If possible prepare it as soon as you get home, but if you need to leave it for a few hours, store it on ice in the fridge to keep it as fresh as possible.

SAUTÉED PURPLE SPROUTING BROCCOLI WITH PANCETTA & SQUID.

I always make the most of the purple sprouting broccoli season (from February to April), as it has a unique flavour and is more appealing than the standard broccoli we get all year round. Here it is blanched then crisped in the fat from the pancetta, which gives it a superb taste. Together with squid, pancetta, garlic and parsley, sprouting broccoli makes a lovely starter – full of wonderful, invigorating flavours. **Serves 4**

200g cleaned squid pouches
  (see page 15)
sea salt and freshly ground black
  pepper
400g purple sprouting broccoli
olive oil for cooking
8 slices of pancetta, halved

Persillade
1 small garlic clove, peeled
5g flat-leaf parsley leaves

Place the squid on a board and cut down one side of each pouch to open it out. Now lightly score the flesh (see below). Slice the scored squid into small pieces.

Bring a large pan of salted water to the boil. Add the broccoli florets and blanch for 2–3 minutes, then drain and plunge into a bowl of iced water to refresh. Once cold, remove from the water, drain and pat dry on kitchen paper. Set aside until ready to use.

Meanwhile, for the persillade, finely chop the garlic and parsley, then chop them together to mix thoroughly; set aside.

Heat a non-stick frying pan over a medium-high heat and add a drizzle of olive oil. Add the pancetta and cook on each side until crispy, then remove from the pan and set aside.

Add the broccoli to the pan with a little more oil and sauté briefly until the florets turn a bit crispy. Remove and set aside.

Now add the squid to the pan, season with salt and pepper and sauté over a medium-high heat for 1–2 minutes. Remove the pan from the heat and return the crispy pancetta and broccoli. Scatter over the persillade, toss together and serve.

Scoring the inside surface of the squid will encourage it to open and curl decoratively as it is seared in the pan. Lay the opened squid pouch on a board with the inside surface uppermost. Score diagonal lines across the flesh, first in one direction, then at right angles to the first lines, cutting about a third of the way through the flesh.

SEARED WOOD PIGEON WITH CELERIAC RÉMOULADE, HAZELNUTS & APPLE.

These days you don't need a specialist game supplier to get hold of wood pigeon, as these tasty birds are now available from selected supermarkets, butchers' and farmers' markets. Celeriac rémoulade is the perfect partner for roasted pigeon breasts, though I also like to serve this delicious, crunchy salad with chicken, quail and cold meats. **Serves 4**

2 wood pigeons
2 rashers of bacon
olive oil for cooking
sea salt and freshly ground black
   pepper

Celeriac rémoulade
200g celeriac
5 tablespoons mayonnaise
   (see page 187)
juice of ½ lemon, or to taste
1 chicory bulb, trimmed
1 red apple
1 green apple
1–2 shallots, peeled and cut into rings
50g hazelnuts, lightly toasted
handful of parsley leaves, chopped

Heat the oven to 180°C/Gas 4. Wrap the pigeons in the bacon rashers and tie with kitchen string to secure. Heat a heavy-based ovenproof frying pan over a medium heat and add a good drizzle of olive oil. Season the wood pigeons all over with salt and pepper. Add to the pan and colour on all sides until golden.

Transfer the pan to the oven and cook the wood pigeons for a further 6 minutes or until cooked to your liking, then leave to rest on a wire rack.

While the pigeons are roasting, prepare the celeriac rémoulade. Peel the celeriac, cut into thin strips and place in a bowl. Toss with the mayonnaise and season with salt, pepper and lemon juice to taste. Slice the chicory into strips. Halve, core and dice the apples. Add the diced apples to the celeriac with the shallots, chicory, hazelnuts and chopped parsley.

Pile the salad onto one side of the serving plates. Unwrap the pigeons, remove the breasts and cut each one into three pieces. Arrange alongside the salad and serve immediately.

HAGGIS, NEEPS & TATTIES.

This is my re-invention of Scotland's national dish. It's very different from the hefty dish of haggis, puréed turnips (neeps) and potatoes traditionally served on Burn's Night! Here the neeps are lightly pickled, the potatoes are fine and crispy, and portions of haggis are fried in breadcrumbs and topped with a quail's egg for an elegant starter. You'll need a Japanese mandoline to cut the potatoes. **Serves 4**

Haggis
500g haggis
2 free-range egg yolks
100g plain flour
1 free-range egg, lightly beaten,
  for coating
100g breadcrumbs
vegetable oil for deep-frying
4 quail's eggs

Neeps
½ turnip (neeps)
1 litre water
150g caster sugar
1 bay leaf
3 thyme sprigs
6 black peppercorns
1–2 garlic cloves
1 teaspoon salt
150ml white wine vinegar

Tatties
1 large potato
20ml clarified butter
sea salt

First prepare the pickled neeps. Peel and thinly slice the turnip. Meanwhile, bring the rest of the ingredients to the boil in a saucepan. Remove from the heat, drop in the turnip slices and leave to infuse for 2–3 hours.

Meanwhile, cook the haggis. Bring a large pot of water to the boil. Wrap the haggis in foil and lower into the pan. When the water comes back to a simmer, turn the heat right down and leave to cook slowly for 2–3 hours.

Once cooked, remove the haggis from the pan, unwrap and slice open. Take it out of the bladder and put into a large bowl. Let cool slightly, then mix in the egg yolks. Turn the haggis out onto a sheet of cling film and shape into a roll, about 5cm in diameter. Wrap in the cling film and refrigerate to firm up.

When ready, remove the pickled neeps from the liquid and cut into thin strips. Set aside.

Once chilled, unwrap the haggis and cut into 2.5cm slices. Put the flour, beaten egg and breadcrumbs into 3 separate containers. Dip the haggis slices first in the flour to coat, then into the beaten egg, and finally into the breadcrumbs to coat all over; set aside.

For the tatties, peel the potato and cut into wafer-thin strips using a Japanese mandoline. Mix with a little clarified butter and salt. Heat a non-stick frying pan, add a quarter of the potato and shape gently into a 5cm circle. Fry gently until crispy, then carefully remove and keep warm while you cook the rest of the potato in the same way to make 4 crispy potato cakes.

To fry the haggis cakes, heat the oil in a deep-fryer or other suitable deep, heavy pan to 180°C. Lower the haggis cakes into the hot oil and fry for 3–4 minutes until golden. Meanwhile, pile the neep strips onto warm plates. Remove the haggis from the pan, drain on kitchen paper and salt lightly.

Add a little more oil to the frying pan and fry the quail's eggs for a minute or until the whites have set but the yolks are soft.

Place the haggis cakes alongside the neeps and top with the quail's eggs. Place the crispy potato on the side and serve at once.

SATURDAY SUPPER

FILLET OF COD WITH HERB BREADCRUMBS, CHORIZO & CLAMS.

I came up with this dish while on holiday in Portugal, where small clams and cockles are so popular. The trick here is to cook them fast and to use the cooking liquid to make the sauce to give that lovely fresh flavour. It's a great way to serve cod, but the technique would work well with any meaty white fish.

Serves 4

250g surf or venus clams in shell
4 chunky portions of cod fillet, about 200g each
150g white bread (ideally day old), crusts removed, torn into chunks
1 tablespoon chopped tarragon
sea salt and freshly ground black pepper
olive oil for cooking
1 tablespoon Dijon mustard
50g chorizo, skinned and roughly chopped
2 garlic cloves, peeled and chopped
50ml white wine
1 tablespoon chopped parsley
a little extra virgin olive oil
12 cherry tomatoes, halved
1 tablespoon chopped basil

Rinse the clams thoroughly under cold running water for 5–10 minutes to remove all grit. Drain and set aside. Have the cod portions ready at room temperature.

For the herb breadcrumbs, put the bread and chopped tarragon into a blender and blitz to fine crumbs; the breadcrumbs will take on a lovely green colour. Tip them into a shallow dish and set aside.

Heat the oven to 180°C/Gas 4. Season the cod portions all over with salt and pepper. Heat a large non-stick ovenproof frying pan over a medium-high heat and add a drizzle of olive oil. When hot, place the cod portions, skin side down, in the pan and cook for 2–3 minutes until the skin starts to crisp.

Transfer the pan to the oven and roast the cod for 4–5 minutes. Take out of the oven and carefully turn the cod skin side up. Using a pastry brush, coat the skin with Dijon mustard. Now dip the skin side into the herb breadcrumbs to coat evenly. Replace the cod portions in the pan, crumbed side up, and bake for a further 1–2 minutes.

While the cod is in the oven, cook the clams. Heat a non-stick sauté pan or deep frying pan and add a drizzle of olive oil. Add the chorizo pieces and cook for 2–3 minutes. Tip in the clams and add the garlic, white wine and chopped parsley. Immediately cover with a tight-fitting lid and cook for 2–3 minutes until the clams steam open.

When the cod portions are cooked, remove them from the oven and set aside to rest in a warm place for a few minutes.

Once the clams are open, remove them with a slotted spoon to a bowl, leaving the chorizo and juices in the pan. Tip in any juices from the rested cod. Bring to the boil and let bubble for a minute or two to reduce the liquor. Add a splash of extra virgin olive oil to thicken it further, along with the cherry tomatoes and basil.

Spoon the sauce over the clams. Divide between warm bowls, placing the cod in the middle.

SEA BASS BAKED IN A SALT CRUST.

This recipe may sound a little scary but it's really very straightforward and a lovely way to cook sea bass in order to retain its wonderful fresh flavour and moist texture. You can prepare the dish ready to bake a few hours ahead, but don't leave the fish sitting in the fridge overnight, as the salt will penetrate the flesh. To serve four, bake two fish, increasing the quantities for the salt crust accordingly. I like to serve the fish with simple accompaniments – new potatoes, pasta or rice and a leafy side salad. **Serves 2**

1 sea bass, about 700g, gutted,
  gills removed and scaled
1 rosemary sprig
1 thyme sprig
3 bay leaves

Salt crust
1kg coarse salt
1kg fine salt
1 tablespoon thyme leaves
2 egg whites, lightly beaten
100ml water

Heat the oven to 200°C/Gas 6. Trim the sea bass if necessary. Open the belly of the fish and place the rosemary and thyme sprigs inside. Using your fingers, tuck up the cavity to stop salt entering and making the flesh salty; set aside.

For the salt crust, put the coarse and fine salt into a large bowl and mix together. Add the thyme leaves, egg whites and water and mix until evenly combined.

Spread about a third of the salt mixture out on a baking tray to form an even layer for the fish to lie on. Place the sea bass on top of the salt. Cover with the remaining salt and pack it around the fish to encase it completely. Now carefully score the salt around the bottom (see below); do this lightly so you don't pierce the skin of the fish. Place in the oven and bake for 30 minutes.

Rest the fish for 5 minutes before serving. For maximum drama, take the fish to the table and carefully open the salt crust with a spatula. This will release a wonderful aroma. Portion the fish and serve with your chosen accompaniments.

Scoring the salt crust lightly around the base with a small, sharp knife before baking will make it much easier to remove once the fish is cooked. After resting the fish, simply run a knife along the score line to open the salt crust. If you don't do this beforehand, it will be very difficult to get into the fish.

MONKFISH POACHED IN A SAFFRON BROTH WITH PEAS & BROAD BEANS.

Visually, this is a truly beautiful dish – impressive to serve when you are entertaining, but deceptively easy to make. Friends and guests at the restaurant often tell me that they are unsure how to poach fish, but it's really not difficult once you know how. Personally, I love the texture of a poached fish, as it is more delicate than the usual pan-fried option. The trick is to get the timing right and make sure the fish is poached through before removing it from the stock. Saffron enhances the flavour of this dish to delicious effect. **Serves 4**

4 pieces of monkfish tail fillet,
    about 150g each
100ml fish stock (see page 185)
pinch of saffron strands
sea salt and freshly ground black
    pepper
30g unsalted butter, in pieces
1 tablespoon whipping cream
200g freshly podded peas
200g freshly podded broad beans,
    skinned
1 teaspoon chopped chives
100g cherry tomatoes, halved
100g baby spinach leaves

When you are ready to cook the monkfish, pour the fish stock into a fairly shallow, heavy-based pan and bring to the boil. Add the saffron strands, lower the heat and simmer gently for 2–3 minutes.

Season the monkfish on both sides with salt and pepper and then carefully lower into the saffron fish stock. Poach very gently for 4–5 minutes on one side, then turn the fillets and cook on the other side for 4–5 minutes; the stock should barely simmer.

To check if your monkfish is cooked, gently insert a needle or fine skewer into the thickest part of the flesh; if it doesn't meet with any resistance, the fish is cooked. Once ready, remove the fish from the pan with a fish slice to a warmed plate; keep warm.

Simmer the poaching liquor until reduced by three-quarters, then whisk in the butter and cream. Add the peas and broad beans and simmer briefly until tender. Add the chives and lastly the tomatoes and baby spinach. Remove from the heat.

To serve, ladle the saffron sauce and vegetables into warmed bowls or deep plates. Slice each monkfish fillet and arrange on top of the vegetables. Serve at once.

SCALLOPS WITH ROASTED, PURÉED & RAW ASPARAGUS.

I like to prepare this during the short asparagus season, as perfectly cooked scallops and asparagus are a great marriage. I'm serving the asparagus in three ways: raw, puréed and roasted, which might seem a bit 'cheffy' but it really makes the most of it. Buy hand-dived scallops if you possibly can. **Serves 4**

2 bunches of asparagus, about 900g in total
olive oil for cooking
½ onion, peeled and thinly sliced
sea salt and freshly ground black pepper
150ml chicken stock (see page 185)
6–8 large scallops in shells, cleaned (see below)

Heat the oven to 180°C/Gas 4. To prepare the asparagus, snap off the woody ends and peel the lower end of the stalks. Divide the asparagus into three equal portions: set aside a third for serving raw, a third for roasting and a third for the purée.

For the purée, finely chop the asparagus. Heat a heavy-based pan over a medium-low heat and add a drizzle of olive oil. Add the onion and sweat gently for 2–3 minutes. Increase the heat, add the chopped asparagus with some seasoning and sweat for 1–2 minutes. Pour on the chicken stock and simmer for 3–4 minutes until the asparagus is cooked. Tip into a blender and blitz to a smooth purée. Transfer to a bowl and cool quickly over a bowl of iced water to preserve the colour, unless serving straight away.

For the roasted asparagus, heat a non-stick ovenproof frying pan over a medium-high heat and add a good drizzle of olive oil. Add the asparagus and sauté for 1–2 minutes. Transfer the pan to the oven and roast for 3–4 minutes until the asparagus is tender.

Meanwhile, thinly slice the raw asparagus spears lengthways and drizzle with olive oil. Once the roasted asparagus is ready, transfer it to a warm plate and set aside.

Halve each scallop horizontally into two discs. Return the frying pan to a high heat and add a good drizzle of olive oil. When hot, place the scallops in the pan, season with salt and pepper and sear them quickly for 45 seconds to 1 minute on each side until golden brown, depending on size. (It is better to leave them slightly underdone than to overcook them, which toughens the flesh.) In the meantime, gently reheat the asparagus purée.

Spoon the asparagus purée onto warm plates and arrange the roasted asparagus and scallops on top. Finish with the raw asparagus and serve at once.

To open scallops, hold with the flatter side uppermost and insert a strong, small knife in between the shells close to the hinge. Twist the knife to break the hinge and open up the shells. Cut through the white muscle to release the scallop meat. Save the coral and skirt to use for sauces; these freeze well, so you can keep them in the freezer until needed.

DUCK BREAST WITH RED ONION, SZECHUAN PEPPER & DRIED APRICOT COMPOTE.

When I'm cooking at home, I always try to find really good alternatives to the time-consuming sauces that we prepare at the restaurant. This tasty compote is a good example – it balances the richness of the duck beautifully and can be prepared well in advance. The Szechuan pepper gives it a unique flavour.

Serves 4

4 duck breasts, with skin, about
   220g each
sea salt and freshly ground black
   pepper
1 red pepper
olive oil for cooking
4 red onions, peeled and halved
   vertically
4 pak choi
2–3 pickled garlic cloves, sliced

Red onion and apricot compote
10g Szechuan pepper
olive oil for cooking
8 red onions, peeled and thinly sliced
100g dried apricots, finely diced
finely grated zest and juice of 1 lemon
300ml chicken stock (see page 185)

First make the compote. Tie the Szechuan pepper in a square of muslin. Heat a heavy-based saucepan over a medium-low heat and add a good drizzle of olive oil, then the sliced onions. Cover and sweat gently for 2–3 minutes. Season with salt and add the dried apricots and pepper pouch. Sweat, covered, for a further 5–6 minutes until the onions are soft. Add the lemon zest and juice, then pour in the chicken stock. Bring to a simmer, turn the heat right down and cook gently, uncovered, for 1 hour until reduced to a compote consistency. Discard the pepper pouch.

Meanwhile, heat the oven to 180°C/Gas 4. Score the skin of the duck breasts and season well with salt, rubbing it into the skin. Set aside.

Spear the red pepper on a fork and turn over a gas burner on the hob until the skin is blackened all over. (Alternatively, scorch the pepper under a hot grill, turning as necessary.) Peel away the skin. Halve the pepper, remove the seeds, then cut into triangles. Keep warm.

Heat a non-stick ovenproof frying pan, add a drizzle of olive oil and place the onion halves in the pan, cut side down. Sweat for a few minutes, then transfer the pan to the oven and cook for 8–10 minutes. Remove to a warm plate and separate the onion layers to make small onion cups. Keep warm.

Heat a non-stick ovenproof frying pan over a medium-high heat and add a little olive oil. Place the duck breasts in the pan, skin side down, and cook for 4–5 minutes until the fat is well rendered. Turn the duck breasts skin side up and place the frying pan in the oven. Roast for 4–5 minutes until the duck is tender but still pink inside. Set aside to rest in a warm place for 5 minutes.

Meanwhile, blanch the pak choi briefly in a pan of boiling salted water until just tender. Drain thoroughly.

Spoon the onion and apricot compote onto warm plates. Halve or thickly slice the duck breasts and place on top of the compote. Garnish with the pickled garlic, red onion cups and red pepper. Serve with the pak choi.

ROASTED PARTRIDGE WITH BRAISED LENTILS & GIROLLES.

Partridge, for me, symbolises the height of the game season. If you are eating game for the first time, this is a great place to start as partridge has a milder flavour than most other game birds. You just need to take care to avoid overcooking it, otherwise the meat will be tough. Check it frequently towards the end of cooking and don't skip the important resting stage. Use the partridge carcasses to make a lovely game stock in the same way as a chicken stock (see page 185). **Serves 4**

4 oven-ready partridges
4 rashers of bacon
olive oil for cooking
50g bacon lardons
2 shallots, peeled and diced
2 carrots, peeled and diced
2 garlic cloves, peeled and chopped
bouquet garni (see page 187)
250g Puy lentils, rinsed and drained
sea salt and freshly ground black pepper
200ml chicken stock (see page 185)
50g butter
100g girolles, cleaned
1 tablespoon sherry vinegar
watercress sprigs to garnish

Heat the oven to 180°C/Gas 4. To prepare the partridges, with a small, sharp knife, cut down either side of the wishbone and remove it. Wrap the bacon rashers around the back of the partridges and tie with string (but not too tightly).

Heat a heavy-based saucepan over a medium-low heat and add a drizzle of olive oil. Add the bacon lardons and cook gently for 2–3 minutes. Add the shallots and carrots and sweat gently for 2–3 minutes, then add the garlic and bouquet garni.

Now add the lentils to the pan and stir to mix with the shallots, carrots and bacon. Season with a little salt and pour on the chicken stock to cover. Bring to a simmer, lower the heat and cook gently for 35–40 minutes, stirring occasionally.

Heat a non-stick ovenproof frying pan over a medium-high heat and add a drizzle of olive oil. Season the partridges all over with salt and pepper and place in the pan. Turn the birds as necessary over the heat for 3–4 minutes until they start to take on a lovely golden colour. Add half of the butter, allow it to melt and foam, then spoon over the birds to baste them.

Once the birds are coloured all over, put the pan into the oven. Roast for 8–10 minutes until the partridges are just cooked. Transfer the birds to a warm plate and leave to rest for 5 minutes.

Add a drizzle of oil to the frying pan and place over a medium-high heat. Add the girolles, season with a little salt and sauté for 1–2 minutes until they release their liquid; drain this off, then sauté the girolles for 30 seconds or so until golden and tender. To finish the lentils, add the sherry vinegar and remaining butter.

Remove the bacon from the birds. Cut off the legs, then, using a sharp knife, take the breasts of the carcasses. Remove the skin from the legs and breasts.

Divide the lentils and girolles between warm serving bowls and arrange the partridge breasts and legs on top. Drizzle over the resting juices from the tray. Garnish with watercress and serve.

SADDLE OF LAMB COOKED ON HAY WITH BOULANGÈRE POTATOES.

Cooking lamb on a bed of hay is a traditional technique revived from old classic cookbooks, which has become a bit of a craze amongst modern chefs. Before the age of the modern oven, smoking meat or fish in this way was one of the easiest ways to get flavours into produce. I love this technique because it epitomises my philosophy of 'from nature to plate'. There is nothing more satisfying than allowing prime produce to be infused by nature itself. (Illustrated on previous pages.) **Serves 4**

1 short saddle of lamb, about 1.5kg
sea salt and freshly ground black
* pepper*
olive oil for cooking
½ bag of hay (clean eating hay from
* the pet shop, not bedding hay)*

To serve
boulangère potatoes (see right)

Heat the oven to 200°C/Gas 6. Lightly score the fat covering the lamb and rub with salt and pepper. Heat a splash of olive oil in a cast-iron casserole dish (with a lid) over a medium heat. Add the saddle of lamb and brown well all over for 6–8 minutes. Remove the lamb from the casserole dish and set aside.

Add the hay to the dish with a little more oil and heat until the hay just starts to smoke. Place the browned saddle of lamb on top of the hay and put the lid on. Cook in the oven for 20–25 minutes until the lamb is pink, or until cooked to your liking.

Lift the lamb from the hay onto a warm platter and leave to rest in a warm place for 5–10 minutes.

Carve the lamb and serve with the boulangère potatoes and French beans or another green vegetable.

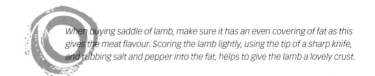
When buying saddle of lamb, make sure it has an even covering of fat as this gives the meat flavour. Scoring the lamb lightly, using the tip of a sharp knife, and rubbing salt and pepper into the fat, helps to give the lamb a lovely crust.

BOULANGÈRE POTATOES.

This is an excellent accompaniment to serve with lamb, especially if you are entertaining, as it can be left to cook by itself in the oven. It's important to get the cooking right. If the stock is bubbling too fast, the top will be crunchy before the potatoes beneath are cooked. If it is too slow, the stock won't reduce and the top won't crisp. **Serves 4**

olive oil for cooking
1 onion, peeled and thinly sliced
1 leek, trimmed, washed and thinly
  sliced
1 fennel bulb, trimmed and thinly
  sliced
2 garlic cloves, peeled and chopped
1 teaspoon fennel seeds
1 teaspoon thyme leaves
300ml lamb stock (see page 186)
  or chicken stock (see page 185)
50g butter
700g potatoes
sea salt and freshly ground black
  pepper

Heat the oven to 160°C/Gas 2–3. Heat a heavy-based frying pan over a medium heat and add a good drizzle of olive oil. Add the onion, leek, fennel and garlic with the fennel seeds and half of the thyme leaves. Sweat for 3–4 minutes, stirring occasionally.

Meanwhile, bring the stock to the boil in a saucepan and add the rest of the thyme leaves. Liberally grease a shallow baking dish with a little of the butter.

Slice the potatoes thinly, using a mandoline (if you have one) or a very sharp knife. Layer the potato slices in the baking dish, overlapping them and alternating the layers with the onion and fennel mixture. Season in between the layers with salt and pepper. Finish with a neat overlapping layer of potato slices.

Pour over the hot stock and dot with the remaining butter. Cover the dish with foil and bake for 1 hour. Remove the foil and cook for another 30 minutes, or until the top is crisp and golden and the potatoes are cooked through.

Leave to stand for a few minutes before serving.

ROLLED ESCALOPE OF VEAL WITH LEMON & CAPER BUTTER.

This is my take on the classic Italian dish. Escalopes are thin pieces of meat, which are beaten out more thinly so they cook really quickly. Buy top-quality veal and take it easy when batting out the escalopes and rolling them around the filling, to ensure they remain intact. When asparagus isn't in season, try using blanched tenderstem or purple sprouting broccoli instead. **Serves 4**

8 asparagus spears
sea salt and freshly ground black
  pepper
4 veal escalopes, about 200g each
4 slices of Parma ham
4 slices of Cheddar (ideally locally
  produced)
4 sage leaves
8 sun-dried tomatoes
olive oil for cooking

Sauce
50g butter
20 small capers, drained and rinsed
1 tablespoon chopped parsley
juice of ½ lemon
6–8 small sage leaves

To prepare the asparagus, snap off the woody ends of the spears and peel the lower end of the stalks. Immerse in a pan of boiling salted water and blanch for 3–4 minutes. Drain and immediately refresh in iced water. Drain and pat dry on kitchen paper.

Place one veal escalope between two sheets of greaseproof paper and flatten slightly, using a meat mallet or rolling pin. Repeat with the other three escalopes. Season them on both sides with salt and pepper. Lay a slice of Parma ham on top of each veal escalope, followed by a slice of cheese, a sage leaf and a sun-dried tomato. Lay two asparagus spears (facing in opposite directions) on top, allowing the tips to extend beyond the edges of the veal.

Now roll each veal escalope around the filling to enclose it completely. Secure at several intervals along the length with kitchen string to hold the escalope together during cooking.

Heat a large non-stick frying pan over a medium-high heat, add a splash of olive oil and fry the rolled veal escalopes for 8–10 minutes, turning them regularly to colour evenly all over. Once cooked, remove to a warm plate and set aside in a warm spot to rest while you prepare the sauce.

To make the sauce, return the pan to the heat, add the butter and allow it to foam. Before it begins to turn brown, add the capers, chopped parsley, lemon juice and sage leaves and remove from the heat.

Place a rolled escalope on each warm plate and spoon over the sauce to serve. Sautéed potatoes are a good accompaniment to this dish.

BEEF WELLINGTON.

Of all the dishes I have made over the years, this is probably the one that's received the most accolades. It is a bit of a lengthy recipe, with several preparation and chilling stages, but each one is important to the end result. You should be able to buy the lacy caul fat or *crépine*, which holds everything together, from a good butcher if you give a few days' notice. It freezes well, so buy enough for another meal and keep it in the freezer. If you are unable to source caul fat, a thin pancake works almost as well.

Beef Wellington is an excellent choice for a larger dinner party and as satisfying to prepare as it is to serve. Just bear in mind that you need to start a day ahead! (Illustrated on previous pages.) **Serves 8**

½ *fillet of beef, about 1.75kg*
1 tablespoon olive oil
sea salt and freshly ground black
  pepper

Mushrooms
2–3 tablespoons olive oil
10g butter
500g button mushrooms, cleaned
  and finely chopped
1 shallot, peeled and finely chopped
1 garlic, peeled and finely chopped
1 teaspoon chopped tarragon

Chicken mousse
1 large skinless chicken breast fillet,
  about 200g, chopped
3 free-range medium egg whites
150ml double cream
150ml whipping cream

To assemble
1 tablespoon olive oil
300g spinach
200g caul fat
100g sliced pancetta
2 sheets of ready-rolled puff pastry ,
  about 35 x 25cm
2 free-range eggs, beaten

Cut the fillet of beef in half lengthways and then wrap both pieces tightly in cling film and chill in the fridge for 24 hours to set the shape.

Unwrap the beef. Heat the 1 tablespoon olive oil in a frying pan until smoking, then add the beef and sear, turning as necessary, for 3–4 minutes until evenly browned on all sides. Allow to cool, then wrap tightly again in cling film and set aside.

For the mushrooms, heat 2 tablespoons olive oil in a frying pan over a low heat and add the butter. Once melted, add the chopped mushrooms and fry gently until very tender. Add the shallot, garlic and tarragon and cook for a further 5–6 minutes, stirring frequently, until the liquid has completely reduced and the pan is quite dry.

For the chicken mousse, put the chopped chicken and egg whites into a food processor and blend until smooth. Pass the mixture through a fine sieve into a large bowl, pushing it through with a spatula. Stir in both creams and season with salt and pepper. To check the seasoning, fry off a teaspoonful of the mixture in a small pan with a little oil, then taste and adjust the uncooked mixture as necessary.

Stir the cooked mushrooms into the chicken mousse, then spoon it into a piping bag fitted with a large plain nozzle (if you have one) and set aside.

Heat 1 tablespoon olive oil in a sauté pan, add the spinach and cook for 1–2 minutes until wilted. Set aside to cool.

Lay out the caul fat on your work surface to form two separate sheets, overlapping the pieces slightly as necessary, then layer the pancetta slices on top. Spoon the wilted spinach across the middle of each pancetta sheet, then pipe or spread the chicken and mushroom mousse on top. Cover both with cling film and chill in the fridge for 1 hour or until set.

Place each piece of seared beef on top of a chicken mousse bed (illustrated on page 132), then lift the caul fat from one side and roll the layers of mousse, spinach, pancetta and caul fat around the beef to form a log. Wrap both logs tightly in cling film and chill in the fridge for 1 hour to set.

Meanwhile, roll out each sheet of puff pastry so that it will be large enough to wrap around a rolled beef fillet and enclose it completely. Set aside to rest for 20 minutes.

Brush the rested pastry with beaten egg. Lay a beef roll along one side of each pastry sheet, then wrap the pastry around the beef, rolling it into a tight cylinder. Fold in the ends, then trim off the excess pastry from the sides and long edge, leaving a slight overlap to seal. Brush the edges with beaten egg and press them against the parcel to seal. Brush the parcels all over with beaten egg (see below) and rest in the fridge for 1 hour.

Heat the oven to 180°C/Gas 4. Brush the parcels again with beaten egg, then sprinkle all over with sea salt. Lift them onto a baking tray and bake for 20–25 minutes, or until the pastry is golden brown all over. Remove from the oven and rest on a warm plate for 5 minutes.

To serve, cut each Beef Wellington into 4 thick slices, discarding the pastry ends. Place a slice on each warm serving plate and season with salt and pepper. Serve at once, with your chosen accompaniments. Sautéed wild mushrooms and wilted spinach or other seasonal greens are ideal accompaniments.

Once you have wrapped the beef roll in the puff pastry, brush the surface of the pastry all over with beaten egg. This seals the pastry and gives it a deep golden sheen once baked.

VEGETABLE PAPILLOTE.

Cooking *en papillote* – in a sealed paper parcel – is such a wonderful way of cooking as it traps the flavours inside. I often cook fish this way, but more recently I've applied the same method to vegetables, cooking them in foil. Make sure the foil doesn't have any holes or the steam and flavours will escape. The parcel should puff out like a balloon in the oven – take it straight to the table for an element of theatre.

Serves 4

Nage

2 carrots, peeled and roughly chopped
1 onion, peeled and roughly chopped
2 celery sticks, roughly chopped
½ fennel bulb, roughly chopped
2 garlic cloves, peeled and halved
finely pared zest of 1 lemon
1 bay leaf
1 thyme sprig

Vegetable papillote

olive oil for cooking
1 carrot, peeled and quartered
1 fennel bulb, trimmed and quartered
8 asparagus spears, trimmed
juice of 1 lemon
6 radishes
1 courgette, quartered lengthways
½ head of broccoli, divided into
   florets
2 baby gem lettuces, halved
   lengthways
1 teaspoon thyme leaves
sea salt
15g butter

For the nage, put all the ingredients into a saucepan and pour on enough cold water to cover. Bring to the boil, lower the heat and simmer for 20 minutes. Remove from the heat and leave to infuse for 10 minutes, then strain the liquor through a fine sieve into a bowl, discarding the vegetables and flavourings. Set aside.

For the papillote, heat the oven to 200°C/Gas 6. Heat a wide, heavy-based pan and add a splash of olive oil. Add the carrot, fennel and asparagus. Pour on enough vegetable nage to cover, add a squeeze of lemon juice and cook over a high heat for 5–6 minutes. Now add the radishes, courgette, broccoli and lettuce and cook for a further 1½ minutes, adding more nage as needed.

Remove the vegetables from the pan with a slotted spoon and set aside. Bring the liquor back to the boil and let bubble to reduce by half. Add the thyme leaves, another squeeze of lemon, a splash of olive oil and a touch of salt. The sauce should have a nice vegetable citrus flavour.

Tear off two large sheets of foil, lay one out on your work surface and fold up the edges. Place a 20cm round of greaseproof paper in the middle and place the vegetables on top of this. Carefully spoon the cooking liquor over the vegetables. Cover with the other sheet of foil and fold the edges together to make a tightly sealed parcel.

Now carefully lift the papillote into an ovenproof sauté pan and place over a medium heat until the foil starts to puff up. Transfer the pan to the oven and cook for 5 minutes. Open the parcel at the table to get the full effect.

WHOLE ROASTED JOHN DORY WITH BRAISED FENNEL, CHIPS & BÉARNAISE SAUCE.

I've found that roasting a whole fish on the bone is a great idea for a Sunday lunch or supper when we have friends over who don't eat meat, but enjoy fish – so-called pescatarians! It's a nice, lighter alternative to the traditional roast joint for everyone else too. I serve it with Béarnaise sauce and chips, and a leafy salad on the side. **Serves 4**

1 large John Dory, about 1kg, cleaned
sea salt and freshly ground black
   pepper
olive oil for cooking
3 thyme sprigs
1 onion, peeled and chopped
3 fennel bulbs, trimmed and chopped
1 teaspoon fennel seeds
1 garlic clove, peeled and finely
   chopped
50ml Pernod
100ml water
1 tablespoon extra virgin olive oil
1 tablespoon chopped dill

Chips
4 medium-large potatoes, such as
   King Edwards
oil for deep-frying

To serve
lemon wedges
Béarnaise sauce (see page 186)

Heat the oven to 180°C/Gas 4. Season the John Dory well all over with salt and pepper, drizzle with a little olive oil and place the thyme sprigs in the belly.

Heat a heavy-based pan over a medium-low heat and add a drizzle of olive oil. Add the chopped onion and fennel and sweat for 3–4 minutes. Scatter over the fennel seeds and garlic and cook for a further 1–2 minutes. Pour in the Pernod, stirring to deglaze, and let bubble to reduce until the pan is dry. Pour in the water, then add the extra virgin olive oil. Cover and cook for 6 minutes until the vegetables are soft. Sprinkle with the chopped dill and set aside.

Place a large heavy-based non-stick frying pan over a medium-high heat, add a little olive oil and place the John Dory in the pan. Cook for 3–4 minutes on each side so that the skin takes on a slight crispness. Transfer the fish to a heavy-based ovenproof dish and place in the oven. Bake for 15 minutes, basting every 5 minutes. Wipe out the frying pan.

Meanwhile, for the chips, peel the potatoes and cut into chips of the required size. Heat the oil in a deep-fryer to 130°C. Pat the potatoes dry with kitchen paper. Lower into the hot oil and fry for 3–4 minutes until soft but with no colour. Remove and drain on kitchen paper.

When the fish has been in the oven for 15 minutes, spoon the fennel and onion mixture around it. Bake for a further 5 minutes or until it is cooked through. To check, insert a needle into the thickest part of the fish and hold it to your lips; it should feel warm. When ready, set aside to rest in a warm place for 5 minutes.

To finish cooking the chips, heat the oil to 180°C. Add the chips and deep-fry for 2–3 minutes until golden brown and crispy. Drain on kitchen paper and season with salt.

Serve the whole roasted fish on a platter accompanied by the chips, lemon wedges and Béarnaise sauce.

ROASTED CHICKEN WITH BRAISED CHICORY WRAPPED IN CRISPY PANCETTA.

It's difficult to beat a classic roast chicken with roast potatoes and seasonal vegetables, but this is a lovely twist for a lighter Sunday roast supper. I always enjoy the contrast of the same vegetable being served cooked and raw on the same plate and it works well here with chicory. Drizzle any juices from the rested chicken over the salad to enhance the balsamic dressing. (Illustrated on previous pages.) **Serves 4**

1 free-range chicken, about 1.4kg
1 lemon
1 large thyme sprig
1 bay leaf
3 garlic cloves, peeled and crushed
25g butter
sea salt and freshly ground/cracked
   black pepper
olive oil for cooking

Mirepoix
1 carrot, peeled and diced
½ leek, trimmed, washed and diced
3 shallots, peeled and diced
2 thyme sprigs
1 bay leaf
2 garlic cloves, peeled

To serve
chicory salad (see right)
braised chicory (see right)

Heat the oven to 180°C/Gas 4. Place the chicken on a board and remove the wishbone (this makes it easier to carve the bird). To do so, lift the skin from the back of the breast and run a sharp knife down either side of the wishbone to release it. Reach in with your fingers and pull out the bone.

Cut the lemon into 8 chunks and place in a bowl with the thyme, bay leaf, garlic and butter and season well. Stuff the lemon and butter mixture into the cavity of the chicken. Now drizzle a little olive oil over the chicken and season well with salt and cracked black pepper.

For the mirepoix, heat a heavy-based frying pan over a medium heat and add a drizzle of olive oil. Add the diced vegetables, thyme, bay leaf and garlic and sweat gently for 2–3 minutes. Transfer to a roasting tray.

Place the chicken on top of the mirepoix and roast in the oven for 50 minutes to 1 hour or until cooked through. To check, insert a needle into the thickest part of the thigh. If the juices run clear, the chicken is cooked.

When the chicken is cooked, lift it onto a warm plate and set aside to rest in a warm place for 10 minutes or so. Discard the mirepoix and spoon off any excess oil from the roasting tray. Put the tray over a medium heat and add a splash of water to deglaze, scraping the bottom of the tray to release any sediment.

Carve the chicken and serve with the chicory salad, braised chicory and the deglazed cooking juices spooned over.

CHICORY SALAD.

Serves 4

4 chicory bulbs (Belgian endive)
1 shallot, peeled
olive oil for cooking
1 tablespoon flat-leaf parsley leaves
1 tablespoon extra virgin olive oil
25ml good-quality balsamic vinegar
sea salt and freshly ground black
pepper

Trim the root end of the chicory bulbs, separate the leaves and place in a bowl. Finely slice the shallot into rings.

Heat a drizzle of olive oil in a small frying pan and gently sweat the shallot for a few minutes to soften.

Scatter the shallot rings and parsley leaves over the chicory and drizzle with the extra virgin olive oil and balsamic vinegar. Season with salt and pepper to taste and toss lightly.

BRAISED CHICORY.

Serves 4

4 chicory bulbs (Belgian endive)
olive oil for cooking
25g butter
sea salt and freshly ground black pepper
squeeze of lemon juice
300ml chicken stock (see page 185)
4 thin slices of pancetta

Heat the oven to 180°C/Gas 4. Trim the root end of the chicory bulbs, keeping them intact. Heat a heavy-based ovenproof pan over a medium-high heat and add a drizzle of olive oil and the butter. Add the chicory bulbs and sweat for 2 minutes, seasoning lightly and adding the lemon juice. Pour on the chicken stock to cover and lay a cartouche on top (see below). Braise in the oven for 30 minutes or until tender when pierced with a small knife.

Drain the chicory on a wire rack, then pat dry with kitchen paper. Wrap each one in a slice of pancetta and secure with a cocktail stick to hold it together.

Heat a non-stick frying pan over a high heat and add a drizzle of olive oil. When hot, add the pancetta-wrapped chicory and turn to colour and crisp the pancetta all around. Transfer to the oven to finish cooking for 8–10 minutes, turning a few times.

Braising the chicory under a cartouche keeps it submerged in the liquid, seals in the flavours and minimises the evaporation of stock. To make a cartouche, cut out a circle of paper that will just fit inside the pan. Fold in half, then into segments, and snip off the point (to make a hole in the middle for steam to escape). Open out the circle of paper and lay on top of the chicory.

ROASTED LEG OF LAMB WITH RATATOUILLE-STUFFED TOMATOES.

This is one of my favourite Sunday roasts. You can't get much more British than a leg of lamb, but serving it in this way gives a certain Mediterranean feel and flavour, which makes the dish seem light and fresh. Infusing the lamb with flavourings like rosemary and fennel seeds makes it deliciously tasty. Most side dishes work with lamb, so choose your vegetables according to the season. You might also like to serve new potatoes alongside here, or a potato gratin (see page 159). **Serves 4**

1.2kg boned and rolled leg of lamb
5 garlic cloves, peeled and chopped
handful of rosemary sprigs, leaves
  only, roughly chopped
1 teaspoon ground cumin
1 teaspoon fennel seeds
sea salt and freshly ground black
  pepper
250ml lamb stock (see page 186)
  or chicken stock (see page 185)
50g butter

Stuffed tomatoes
4 large tomatoes on the vine
olive oil for cooking
1 onion, peeled and diced
3 garlic cloves, peeled and finely
  chopped
1 tablespoon dried herbs de Provence
1 courgette, diced
1 aubergine, diced
1 red pepper, cored, deseeded and
  diced

Place the lamb on a board. In a bowl, mix together the garlic, rosemary, cumin and fennel seeds. Using a sharp knife, pierce little slits all over the surface of the lamb. Using your fingers, push the rosemary and spice mixture into the cuts. Season the meat with salt and pepper. Put to one side.

To prepare the tomatoes, snip them off the vine, but leave the stalks intact. Cut a slice off the top off the tomatoes, removing about a quarter, and reserve these lids. Using a teaspoon, carefully scoop out the juice and seeds from inside, leaving the shells intact; set aside, along with the tops.

For the ratatouille stuffing, heat a heavy-based saucepan over a medium heat and add a little olive oil. Add the onion and cook slowly for 3–4 minutes. Stir in the garlic and dried herbs. Now turn up the heat and add the courgette, aubergine and some salt and pepper. Cook, stirring often, for a further 3–4 minutes; you may need to add more olive oil as the aubergine will absorb quite a lot. Add the red pepper and cook for a further 2–3 minutes, stirring occasionally. Check the seasoning and take off the heat.

To cook the lamb, heat the oven to 180°C/Gas 4. Heat a heavy-based ovenproof pan over a medium-high heat and add a little olive oil. Add the lamb joint and colour on all sides, allowing 3–4 minutes. Transfer to the oven and roast for 15 minutes.

Meanwhile, fill the tomatoes with the ratatouille and put the lids back on. Stand the stuffed tomatoes in a small roasting tray. Add the stock, butter and a drizzle of olive oil to the tray.

When the meat has been roasting for 15 minutes, turn the setting down to 160°C/Gas 3 and put the stuffed tomatoes into the oven. Roast the meat for a further 20 minutes, along with the tomatoes, basting these with the pan juices from time to time.

Rest the lamb in a warm place for 10 minutes. Slice the meat and serve with the stuffed tomatoes, spooning over all the pan juices.

ROASTED LOIN OF PORK WITH SAVOY CABBAGE, APPLE & CHESTNUTS.

In all honesty, it's the crackling that I enjoy most with roast pork. I love its salty crunch and the contrast with the tender roast meat. Savoy cabbage flavoured with apple, chestnuts and bacon is the perfect match for this roast. **Serves 6**

1.5kg boned and rolled pork loin
sea salt and freshly ground black
  pepper
olive oil for cooking
1 medium Savoy cabbage, trimmed
100g bacon lardons
3 carrots, peeled and diced
½ celeriac, peeled and diced
1 garlic clove, peeled and chopped
200ml water
100g cooked peeled chestnuts
2 apples

Heat the oven to 230°C/Gas 8 and put a roasting tray inside to heat up. Meanwhile season the joint of pork all over with salt and pepper, rubbing the salt into the skin. Place the hot roasting tray over a medium heat on the hob, add a drizzle of olive oil, then add the pork and colour all over for 4–5 minutes.

Turn the pork skin side up and transfer to the hot oven. Roast for 10 minutes. Lower the oven setting to 180°C/Gas 4 and roast for a further 45 minutes or until the pork is almost cooked through.

Meanwhile, remove any coarse dark green outer leaves from the cabbage. Separate the leaves and cut out the tough vein from each leaf. Shred the cabbage finely and set aside.

Turn the oven setting up to 220°C/Gas 7 and roast the pork for a final 5 minutes to get the crackling crispy and golden. Remove from the oven and set aside to rest for 10–15 minutes.

While the crackling is crisping, heat a heavy-based sauté pan over a medium heat and add a drizzle of oil. Add the bacon lardons and cook for 3–4 minutes until they start to crisp. Now add the carrots and celeriac with a little salt and lower the heat. Cover and sweat gently for 4–5 minutes to soften without colouring.

Add the shredded cabbage to the pan with the garlic and sweat gently for a further 2–3 minutes. Pour in the water, turn up the heat and put the lid back on. Cook for 3–4 minutes until the cabbage is almost tender.

Meanwhile, peel, core and dice the apples (to the same size as the carrots and celeriac). Add to the cabbage with the chestnuts and cook for a further 2 minutes until the cabbage is cooked.

To serve, slice the pork and arrange on warm plates with the cabbage, making sure everyone gets a portion of crackling too. Pour over any resting juices from the pork.

ROASTED RIB OF BEEF WITH YORKSHIRE PUDDINGS & HORSERADISH CREAM.

Roast beef and Yorkshire pudding has to be one of the nation's best-loved dishes. The most vital secret to success here is to buy a really top-quality piece of beef. It's a rare treat these days, so why not splash out… Make sure the oven is nice and hot when you put the beef in, to ensure it develops a lovely crust before you turn the heat down. And after cooking, rest the meat for a full 20 minutes to allow it to relax and ensure it will be juicy and succulent when you carve it. (Illustrated on previous pages.) **Serves 6**

3kg rib of beef on the bone
vegetable oil for cooking
sea salt
2 tablespoons freshly cracked pepper
4 large potatoes, peeled and halved
150ml chicken stock (see page 185)

To serve
Yorkshire puddings (see right)
horseradish cream (see right)

Heat the oven to its highest setting (probably 240°C/Gas 9). Put a large roasting tray into the oven to heat up. Meanwhile, season the rib of beef well with salt and the cracked pepper, rubbing the seasoning into the meat.

Place the roasting tray over a medium-high heat on the hob and add a drizzle of oil. Place the rib of beef in the roasting tray and colour all over, turning as necessary. This may take 8–10 minutes but it's very important not to skimp on this stage.

Now add the potatoes to the tray and turn to colour on all sides. Transfer the roasting tray to the very hot oven and roast for 15 minutes. This allows the beef to take on colour quickly and will create a lovely crust.

Reduce the oven setting to 180°C/Gas 4 and roast for a further 30 minutes or until the beef is cooked to your liking. To check, insert a needle into the thickest part for 30 seconds, then remove and place to your lip. If the needle is slightly warm, the meat is ready to come out if you want it pink. If it's hot or very hot it will be medium to well done. If it is cold, it needs longer in the oven.

When the beef is ready, transfer it and the potatoes to a warm platter and set aside to rest in a warm place for about 20 minutes. Pour off any fat from the roasting tray into a bowl (save to use to roast potatoes another day). Place the tray over a medium heat and add the chicken stock, stirring to deglaze and scrape up the tasty sediment from the bottom of the pan to make a light gravy.

Carve the beef and serve with the roast potatoes, a seasonal green vegetable or two, Yorkshire puddings and horseradish cream.

YORKSHIRE PUDDINGS.

At home Yorkshire puddings are a 'must-have' whenever we have roast beef. I have my legendary friend John Hardwick from Sheffield to thank for this recipe. It is exceptionally good. Don't be tempted to open the oven door to check on the puddings while they are baking or they will collapse. **Serves 6**

115g plain flour
2 free-range large eggs
125ml milk
⅔ teaspoon salt
freshly ground black pepper
4 tablespoons beef dripping (from the roasting joint) or vegetable oil

Heat the oven to 220°C/Gas 7 and put a baking tray inside to heat up. Put the flour into a mixing bowl and make a well in the middle. Add the eggs with half of the milk and beat until smooth. Now add the rest of the milk and season with the salt and a grind of pepper, mixing well. Leave the batter to stand for 3–4 hours.

Spoon about 1 tablespoon beef fat or vegetable oil into each compartment of a non-stick 6-hole Yorkshire pudding tray. Slide the tray onto the hot baking tray in the oven and heat for 5 minutes or until smoking hot.

Now quickly ladle the batter into the tray to three-quarters fill each compartment. Immediately return to the oven and bake for 20 minutes or until well puffed and golden brown. Serve at once.

HORSERADISH CREAM.

This traditional roast beef accompaniment tastes so much better if it is made with fresh horseradish. You can buy this from farmers' markets and some supermarkets, or better still, grow your own and pick it to grate fresh from the garden. **Serves 6**

250ml whipping cream
1 teaspoon red wine vinegar
1 tablespoon freshly grated horseradish
1 teaspoon crème fraîche
sea salt

Whip the cream in a bowl until it holds firm peaks, then add the wine vinegar and whisk briefly to incorporate. Fold in the grated horseradish and crème fraîche and season with salt to taste.

ROASTED RACK OF VENISON WITH SPICED RED CABBAGE.

This is something a bit different to serve as a Sunday roast. I've always loved venison and the gamey flavour of the lean meat with the spiced red cabbage is a marriage made in heaven. I often buy local foragers' home-made preserves from our local farmers' market to serve with venison – redcurrant jelly, elderberry jam and rowanberry jelly are especially good. **Serves 4**

1kg rack of roe deer venison on the bone
vegetable oil for cooking
sea salt and freshly ground black pepper
50g butter
1 thyme sprig

Spiced red cabbage
½ medium-large red cabbage
olive oil for cooking
½ onion, peeled and sliced
2 star anise
1 cinnamon stick
pared zest and juice of 1 orange
50g soft light brown sugar
50ml white wine vinegar
400ml red wine
100ml port
50g sultanas
1 dessert apple

To serve
redcurrant or rowanberry jelly

First, prepare the cabbage. Cut out the core and finely shred the cabbage. Heat a heavy-based saucepan over a medium heat and add a generous drizzle of olive oil. Add the onion and sweat for 2–3 minutes, then add the cabbage and cook for 1–2 minutes. Add the star anise, cinnamon and some salt and pepper and cook for another 1–2 minutes to release the flavours.

Now add the orange zest and sprinkle in the sugar. Add the orange juice and wine vinegar and let bubble to reduce down. Pour in the red wine and port. Add the sultanas and leave to cook gently for 40 minutes. Peel, core and dice the apple. Add to the cabbage, toss to mix and set aside.

Meanwhile, for the venison, heat the oven to 200°C/Gas 6. Heat a large non-stick ovenproof frying pan over a medium heat and add a drizzle of oil. Season the venison joint on both sides with salt and pepper and place in the hot pan. Colour the meat well on all sides, for about 3 minutes. Add the butter to the pan and let it melt and foam, then add the thyme and baste the joint with the foaming butter.

Transfer the pan to the oven. Roast the venison for 15 minutes, then check; the meat should still be pink inside. Transfer to a warm platter and leave to rest in a warm place for 10 minutes. Save any juices in the pan.

Slice the venison and arrange on warm plates with the braised cabbage. Reheat any pan juices and drizzle over the meat. Add a spoonful of redcurrant jelly and a sprinkling of pepper to serve.

EXTRA ACCOMPANIMENTS

COLCANNON.

I serve this comforting mashed potato and cabbage dish with various roasts, especially in the winter. For a full-flavoured mash, bake the potatoes on rock salt, rather than boil them, if you have time. **Serves 4**

1kg potatoes
sea salt and freshly ground black
   pepper
200g Savoy cabbage, trimmed
olive oil for cooking
50g bacon lardons
1 garlic clove, peeled and chopped
100ml milk
freshly grated nutmeg
75g butter
8 spring onions, trimmed and
   finely sliced
1 teaspoon chopped parsley

Peel and quarter the potatoes and boil in salted water until tender, then drain well. Meanwhile, shred the cabbage finely.

Heat a heavy-based sauté pan over a medium heat and add a drizzle of olive oil. Add the lardons and sweat for 3–4 minutes, then add the cabbage and cook over a medium-low heat for 2–3 minutes. Add the garlic and half a cupful of water. Cover and cook for 5–6 minutes until the cabbage is tender.

When the potatoes are nearly cooked, bring the milk to the boil and grate in a little nutmeg. Mash the potatoes in a pan, then slowly incorporate the milk and butter. Season to taste.

Drain the cabbage, then fold through the mashed potato with the spring onions, parsley and a twist of pepper. Serve at once.

PUMPKIN & PARMESAN GRATIN.

This is an ideal complement to an autumnal Sunday roast, but it can also be served as a vegetarian main course with roasted pumpkin or roasted autumn vegetables on the side. **Serves 4**

600g pumpkin
olive oil to drizzle
sea salt and freshly ground black
   pepper
2 onions, peeled
1 bay leaf
1 clove
25g butter, plus a knob
2 garlic cloves, peeled and chopped
4 sage leaves, shredded
400ml milk
25g plain flour
100g Parmesan, freshly grated
½ teaspoon Dijon mustard
2 egg yolks

Heat the oven to 180°C/Gas 4. Cut the pumpkin into wedges, removing the seeds but leaving the skin on. Put on a baking tray, drizzle with olive oil and season with salt and pepper. Bake for 40 minutes or until tender. Let cool slightly, then cut the pumpkin flesh from the skin and chop into cubes. Place in a baking dish.

Slice 1 onion; stud the other one with the bay leaf and clove. Heat a small heavy-based frying pan over a low heat and add the knob of butter, followed by the sliced onion, garlic and sage. Sweat gently for 5–6 minutes, then spoon over the pumpkin.

Meanwhile, bring the milk to the boil in a pan with the studded onion. Take off the heat and set aside to infuse. In a separate pan, melt the 25g butter, then stir in the flour and cook, stirring, for 2–3 minutes to make a roux. Strain the milk and slowly stir into the roux. Cook, stirring, for 4–5 minutes, then take off the heat. Stir in the Parmesan and mustard, then the egg yolks. Pour the sauce over the pumpkin. Bake for 10–12 minutes until golden.

KOFFMANN'S POTATO GRATIN.

I often serve this on the table with my Sunday roast. My mentor, Pierre Koffmann, taught me the secrets of a good potato gratin when I was working for him in London. The trick is to ensure that the potatoes are sliced very thinly, then salted and squeezed to get rid of excess starch. Cooking the gratin slowly in a low oven develops the flavours and gives that lovely homely golden topping. **Serves 4**

8 large potatoes
sea salt and freshly ground black
* pepper*
500ml whipping cream
freshly grated nutmeg
10g butter
1 garlic clove, halved

Heat the oven to 140°C/Gas 1. Peel the potatoes and cut them into wafer-thin slices, using a very sharp knife, or better still, a mandoline if you have one. Place in a colander to drain. Sprinkle the potato slices lightly with salt and leave to sit in the colander for 10–12 minutes.

Meanwhile, slowly bring the cream to just below the boil in a deep pan over a low heat. Season lightly with salt and pepper and grate in a little nutmeg.

Grease a large, shallow ovenproof dish with the butter and rub with the cut surface of the garlic clove.

Squeeze the potato slices to remove excess liquid and layer them in the prepared dish. Slowly pour over the hot cream to just cover the potatoes.

Bake in the oven for 50 minutes to 1 hour until golden on top and cooked through. Check the potatoes are cooked by inserting a small knife in the centre; it should pass through the layers easily. Serve hot.

Illustrated on previous pages:
Colcannon (top left); Pumpkin & Parmesan gratin
(bottom left); Koffmann's potato gratin (right)

COURGETTE & AUBERGINE FILO TARTS.

I love to serve these tarts as an accompaniment to roast lamb, but it's also a good recipe to have up your sleeve for a starter. Or you can serve a couple of them with a salad and rustic bread as a vegetarian main course. Vary the vegetables according to the season, and as you fancy. **Makes 9**

50g butter, melted
250g packet ready-made filo pastry
olive oil for cooking
1 aubergine, sliced
sea salt and freshly ground black
  pepper
1 teaspoon ground cumin
2 courgettes, sliced
1 garlic clove, peeled and sliced
100g cherry tomatoes, halved
1 tablespoon chopped basil, plus
  a few torn leaves to finish
1 tablespoon chopped black olives
100g mozzarella, diced
1 teaspoon dried herbes de Provence

Heat the oven to 180°C/Gas 4. Brush a 9-hole non-stick Yorkshire pudding tray with melted butter.

Lay one filo sheet on a board and brush with melted butter, then place another sheet of filo pastry on top and brush with butter again. Cut out 12cm squares and use a pair of filo squares to line each mould. Repeat this process to line the remaining moulds. Bake in the oven for 5 minutes until golden.

Meanwhile, heat a non-stick frying pan over a medium heat and add a generous drizzle of olive oil. When hot, add the aubergine slices, season with salt and pepper and sprinkle with the cumin. Cook, turning as necessary, until slightly golden on both sides, then remove to a sieve with a slotted spoon and leave to drain.

Heat a little more oil in the pan, then add the courgette slices and cook, turning to colour both sides, for 3–4 minutes. Remove and place with the aubergine to drain off excess oil.

Put the aubergine and courgette into a large bowl. Add the garlic, cherry tomato halves, chopped basil and olives and toss together.

Now divide the vegetable filling evenly between the filo cases. Top with the mozzarella and sprinkle with the dried herbs. Bake for 6–8 minutes until the mozzarella is melted and bubbling. Serve scattered with a few torn basil leaves.

SIMPLE DESSERTS

PANNA COTTA WITH BLUEBERRY COMPOTE.

This dessert is incredibly easy to make. The important thing is to get the texture just right – smooth, silky and not too firm – so it is vital to use the correct amount of gelatine. Buttermilk gives this panna cotta a lovely sharpness, but you can substitute milk if you like. **Serves 4–6**

a little sunflower oil for oiling
2 sheets of leaf gelatine, 4g each
150ml whipping cream
½ vanilla pod, split and seeds scraped
finely pared zest and juice of ½ lemon
40g caster sugar
180ml buttermilk

Blueberry compote
250g blueberries, washed
1 tablespoon lemon juice
40g sugar, or to taste

To finish (optional)
150g shelled cobnuts

Lightly oil 4–6 non-stick dariole or other small moulds, about 3.5cm in diameter and 5cm deep. Soften the gelatine leaves in a dish of very cold water for 10 minutes.

Meanwhile, pour the cream into a heavy-based pan and add the vanilla pod and seeds, lemon zest and sugar. Heat slowly over a low heat and then simmer gently for 5 minutes.

Remove the pan from the heat. Immediately squeeze the gelatine leaves to remove excess water and add them to the hot cream mixture, stirring until fully dissolved.

Pass the mixture through a fine sieve into a shallow container. Refrigerate until cooled to just warm, but not set.

Finally, whisk in the buttermilk, followed by the lemon juice. Transfer the panna cotta mixture to a jug and pour evenly into the prepared moulds. Chill for 4–6 hours, or until set.

In the meantime, if including cobnuts, finely slice them using a mandoline if you have one and toast in a preheated oven at 180°C/Gas 4 for 3–4 minutes until golden. Tip the nuts onto a plate and leave to cool.

For the compote, put the blueberries, lemon juice and sugar into a small pan and cook over a medium-high heat for 3–5 minutes until the berries start to burst and release their juice. Taste for sweetness, adding more sugar if needed. Cool slightly.

To unmould each panna cotta, briefly dip the base of the mould in hot water and upturn into a shallow bowl – the panna cotta should be released quite easily. Surround with the blueberry compote and finish with the toasted cobnuts, if using.

RHUBARB CRUMBLE TARTS.

A good crumble is the perfect way to round off a Sunday lunch and surely one of Britain's most popular puddings. I do variations of crumble throughout the year, such as apple, greengage, rhubarb and red berry, according to the season, and I'm particularly fond of this rolled oatmeal topping, which works with any fruit. **Serves 4**

Pastry

250g plain flour, plus extra for dusting
50g icing sugar
150g unsalted butter, in pieces
1 free-range medium egg
1 free-range medium egg yolk,
  lightly beaten

Rhubarb filling

6 rhubarb stalks, de-strung if
  necessary and cut into 1cm lengths
180g sugar, or to taste
finely grated zest and juice of 1 orange

Crumble topping

250g plain flour
pinch of sea salt
200g cold unsalted butter, in pieces
200g soft light brown sugar
75g rolled oats (or oatmeal)
few drops of pink food colouring
lemon thyme or shredded mint
  to finish (optional)

To make the pastry, sift the flour and icing sugar together into a food processor. Add the butter and pulse until the mixture resembles breadcrumbs. Add the whole egg and pulse briefly until the dough just comes together. Turn out onto a lightly floured surface, knead gently, then flatten into a round. Wrap in cling film and chill for 30 minutes.

In the meantime, for the filling, put the rhubarb into a heavy-based saucepan with the sugar and orange zest and juice. Bring to a simmer, lower the heat and cook gently for 10–15 minutes until the rhubarb is softened but still holding its shape.

Meanwhile, to make the crumble, sift the flour and salt into a bowl. Add the butter and rub in with your fingertips until the mixture resembles coarse crumbs. Stir in the brown sugar, oats and a little food colouring – to give the crumble a nice pastel pink colour. Cover and chill for 20 minutes.

Roll out the pastry on a lightly floured surface to a 3–4mm thickness and use to line 4 individual flan tins, 7.5cm in diameter and 2.5cm deep. Trim the excess pastry away from the edges. Place in the fridge to rest for 15 minutes before baking. Heat the oven to 180°C/Gas 4.

Line the pastry cases with baking parchment and add a layer of baking beans. Bake the pastry cases 'blind' for 10 minutes, then remove the paper and beans and bake for a further 10 minutes until the pastry is cooked through. Remove the paper and beans and brush the inside of the hot pastry cases with the beaten egg yolk to seal. Set aside on a wire rack.

Scatter the crumble on a baking tray and bake for 6–8 minutes until golden and crispy.

To serve, warm the rhubarb compote, if necessary, and use to fill the tart cases. Scatter the crumble evenly over the surface. Finish with a sprinkling of herbs or leave plain if you prefer. Serve with a scoop of vanilla ice cream or pouring cream.

PEARS POACHED IN CHOCOLATE.

This is an ideal dinner party dessert as you can prepare it in advance and have it ready to serve before your guests even arrive. I just love the simple elegance of the glossy, coated pears sitting in their pool of chocolate sauce. The secret is to ensure the pears are properly poached so that when you tuck in, the spoon goes in easily. **Serves 4**

4 medium ripe pears, preferably Comice, Williams or another roundish variety

Poaching liquor
400ml water
100g caster sugar
100g good-quality dark chocolate (70% cocoa solids), in pieces
juice of ½ lemon

For the poaching liquor, put the water, sugar, chocolate and lemon juice into a medium heavy-based saucepan. Heat gently, stirring occasionally, until the chocolate is completely melted, then allow to simmer for 10 minutes.

Meanwhile, carefully peel the pears, keeping their shape and leaving the stems intact. Scoop out the core and seeds from the base (see below). Cut a thin sliver off the bases so the pears will stand upright.

To poach the pears, gently lower them into the simmering poaching liquid. Cover with a piece of parchment paper and weight down with a heatproof plate that fits inside the pan, to keep them submerged. Poach gently for 30–40 minutes, or until the pears are just soft, but retaining their shape.

Using a slotted spoon, lift the cooked pears out of the pan onto a warm plate. Increase the heat to medium and let the poaching liquor bubble steadily until reduced to a glossy chocolate sauce with a syrupy consistency.

Serve the warm pears with the hot chocolate sauce poured over and a scoop of vanilla ice cream on the side.

The easiest and neatest way to core whole pears for poaching is to use a melon baller. Working from the base, press the melon baller into the middle of the pear, turn it and remove to scoop out the core and seeds.

PRUNE CLAFOUTIS.

There is something special about classic French desserts like clafoutis. Here I have put prunes inside, but you can equally use figs, blueberries or cherries. The clafoutis is best served still warm. **Serves 4**

a little butter for greasing
250g pitted prunes
200ml milk
200ml double cream
4 free-range medium eggs, lightly
    beaten
1 vanilla pod, split and seeds scraped
75g plain flour
pinch of sea salt
120g caster sugar
icing sugar for dusting

Heat the oven to 150°C/Gas 2. Lightly butter a 23cm baking dish or 4 individual baking dishes, about 10cm in diameter. Scatter the prunes evenly over the bottom of the dish(es). Combine the milk, cream, eggs and vanilla seeds in a jug.

Mix the flour, salt and sugar together in a large bowl, form a well in the centre and slowly pour in the liquid, whisking as you do so, to form a smooth batter. Or use a blender – it's faster.

Pour the batter over the prunes and bake until slightly puffed and golden but still soft in the centre; allow about 25 minutes for a large clafoutis, 15 minutes for individual ones. Leave to stand for 10 minutes before serving, dusted with icing sugar.

RED FRUIT CONSOMMÉ.

This dessert looks impressive but it's easy and can be prepared ahead. Put your berries in serving bowls and have the consommé ready to pour over. (Illustrated on previous pages.) **Serves 4**

Red fruit consommé
400g strawberries
400g raspberries
200g caster sugar
juice of ½ lemon
100ml water

To serve
100g blueberries
100g blackberries
100g strawberries, halved or quartered
    if large
100g raspberries
handful of mint leaves, cut into strips

For the fruit consommé, put the strawberries, raspberries, sugar, lemon juice and water into a heavy-based pan. Quickly bring to the boil, then lower the heat and simmer gently for 3–4 minutes until the berries release lots of juice. Remove from the heat and set aside to cool slightly, for 5 minutes.

Lay a large dampened muslin cloth over a large bowl, leaving plenty overhanging the sides. Carefully tip the berries and juice into the muslin and bring the corners of the muslin together over the bowl. Tie with string, leaving a length to tie onto an overhanging hook (or perhaps the door handle of a wall kitchen cupboard), suspending the muslin bag over the bowl. Leave to drip naturally for about 1½ hours until all the consommé has passed through; don't be tempted to squeeze the muslin or the consommé will lose its clarity. Cover and chill until required.

To serve, divide the fresh berries between individual dishes or soup plates, pour the fruit consommé around the fruit and sprinkle with the shredded mint.

PAIN PERDU WITH ROASTED FIGS.

Pan perdu is one of those desserts that can be thrown together at a moment's notice. Here I've served it topped with honey-roasted figs, but you can use almost any fruit in season – try pan-roasted apple or pear wedges, lightly poached berries, or even roasted bananas. If you happen to have any leftover brioche, use this in place of bread for a luxury version. Pain perdu is always best served as soon as it's assembled, before the bread has time to go soggy. **Serves 4**

Roasted figs

8 ripe figs
40ml runny honey
20g unsalted butter
juice of ½ orange
pinch of ground cinnamon

Pain perdu

4 free-range large eggs
275ml milk (or half milk, half cream)
2 tablespoons caster sugar
4 tablespoons runny honey
finely grated zest of ½ orange
1 vanilla pod, split and seeds scraped
½ teaspoon ground cinnamon
4 slices of white bread
1 tablespoon vegetable oil
20g unsalted butter
icing sugar for dusting

To finish (optional)

handful of toasted almonds

For the roasted figs, heat the oven to 180°C/Gas 4. Put the honey, butter, orange juice and cinnamon into a small saucepan and heat gently until melted and combined.

Place the figs on a baking tray and spoon the honey and orange mixture over them. Roast, basting frequently with the juices, for 10–15 minutes, until the figs are tender. Using a slotted spoon, transfer the figs to a dish.

Pour the honey and orange sauce from the tray into a small pan and let bubble to reduce until thickened slightly. Halve the figs and spoon over the sauce to glaze.

Lower the oven setting to 120°C/Gas ½. For the pain perdu, in a large bowl, whisk together the eggs, milk, sugar, 1 tablespoon of the honey, the orange zest, vanilla seeds and cinnamon. Pour the mixture into a deep plate (or shallow dish).

In batches as necessary, lay the bread slices in the egg mixture and leave to soak for 2–3 minutes, turning once. Meanwhile, in a non-stick frying pan, heat the oil and butter until hot. Add the soaked bread slices and fry for about 2–3 minutes, turning once, until golden brown on both sides. Transfer to a plate or baking tray and keep warm while you fry the rest.

To serve, dust the pain perdu with icing sugar. Place on warm plates and top with the roasted figs and sauce. Drizzle with the remaining honey and scatter over a few toasted almonds if you like. Serve at once.

PAVLOVA WITH RASPBERRIES, PEACHES & LIME MASCARPONE CREAM.

This is such a lovely mouth-watering dessert. It can be filled with any seasonal fruit, from red berries, through pineapple and passion fruit to poached rhubarb, but my favourite way to enjoy it is with raspberries and peaches at the height of summer. Typically, the soft-centred meringue is topped with whipped cream, but instead I'm using a fresh lime mascarpone cream. **Serves 6–8**

Meringue
6 large egg whites
1½ teaspoons white wine vinegar
250g caster sugar
1 teaspoon cornflour

Lime mascarpone cream
250ml whipping cream
50g icing sugar
150g mascarpone
finely grated zest of 1 lime

To finish
3 ripe peaches
finely grated zest and juice of 1 lime
30g caster sugar, or to taste
500g raspberries
1 tablespoon finely shredded mint

Heat the oven to 110°C/Gas ¼. Line a large baking sheet with baking parchment. To make the meringue, using an electric mixer or electric hand whisk, whisk the egg whites with the wine vinegar until they begin to froth and increase in volume. Now whisk in two-thirds of the sugar, a little at a time. When stiff peaks form, add the remaining sugar and sift in the cornflour. Fold in, using a large metal spoon, until just incorporated.

Spoon the meringue into a mound in the centre of the baking sheet. Using the back of the spoon, flatten the meringue into a large disc, beginning at the centre and working toward the edge. Make the edge of the meringue slightly higher to create a hollow for the filling to sit in. Bake for 1½–2 hours, until crispy on the outside and still soft in the middle. The meringue should be a light golden colour. Set aside to cool completely.

Meanwhile, make the lime mascarpone cream. Whisk the cream and icing sugar together in a bowl to form soft peaks. In another large bowl, stir the mascarpone and lime zest together. Fold in the whipped cream, using a large metal spoon, keeping as much volume as possible. Cover and refrigerate.

Halve and stone the peaches, then cut into wedges and place in a bowl. Add the lime zest and juice, and the sugar. Toss together, then add the raspberries and mint and mix gently. Taste and add more sugar if needed, depending on the sweetness of the berries. They should begin to release their juice, forming a sort of sauce.

To serve the pavlova, fill the centre of the meringue with the lime mascarpone cream. Pile the raspberries and peaches on top.

The addition of a little cornflour and vinegar to a classic French meringue gives a pavlova its unique characteristics: a deliciously chewy, marshmallowy texture within a crisp crust. It is important to whisk the meringue until it is stiff before folding in the sifted cornflour and last of the sugar. If the meringue is too soft the pavlova won't have the required depth and desired texture.

CARROT CAKE WITH CREAM CHEESE TOPPING

I fell in love with this cake when my pastry chef started making small petit four versions at the restaurant. I brought some home for the kids and the recipe has since become a family favourite. **Makes 12**

a little butter for greasing
190g plain flour
1½ teaspoons baking powder
½ teaspoon bicarbonate of soda
1 teaspoon ground cinnamon
¾ teaspoon freshly grated nutmeg
95g desiccated coconut
4 free-range medium eggs
135ml vegetable oil
190g soft dark brown sugar
400g peeled carrots, grated

Topping

270g cream cheese
230g icing sugar, sifted
160g unsalted butter, softened
1 vanilla pod, split and seeds scraped,
  or 1 teaspoon vanilla extract
handful of pistachio nuts, chopped,
  to finish

Heat the oven to 180°C/Gas 4. Grease and line a 30 x 20cm baking tin with baking parchment. Sift the flour with the baking powder, bicarbonate of soda and spices into a large bowl. Stir in the desiccated coconut.

Using an electric mixer or electric hand whisk, whisk the eggs, oil and brown sugar together until fluffy and thick. Using a large, metal spoon, carefully fold in the flour and coconut mixture until just combined. Finally, add the grated carrots and fold in gently.

Spoon the mixture into the prepared tin, spreading it evenly and into the corners. Bake for 20–25 minutes until a fine skewer or cocktail stick inserted into the centre of the cake comes out clean.

Leave the cake in the tin for 10 minutes, then transfer to a wire rack to cool completely.

To make the topping, beat the cream cheese, icing sugar, butter and vanilla seeds or extract together, using the mixer or electric whisk, for at least 5 minutes until the mixture is fluffy and white.

Cut the cake into squares and top each one with a generous spoonful of the cream cheese mixture. Finish with a sprinkling of chopped pistachios.

WHISKY BABAS WITH BERRIES.

This is my take on the classic rum baba. Being Scottish, I like to make the syrup with whisky instead of rum, but you can flavour it with other alcohol if you like – orange juice with a dash of Grand Marnier or other orange liqueur perhaps. The babas freeze really well, so you can make them well ahead or freeze any you don't need now; defrost them before soaking in the syrup. **Makes 10**

Babas

3 tablespoons milk

5g active dried yeast

200g strong white bread flour,
   plus extra for dusting

6g sea salt

20g caster sugar

2 free-range medium eggs,
   lightly whisked

60g butter, softened, plus extra
   for greasing

Whisky syrup

200g sugar

200ml water

200ml whisky, or to taste

1 vanilla pod, split and seeds scraped

finely grated zest of 1 orange

finely grated zest of 1 lemon

Chantilly cream

300ml whipping cream

25g icing sugar

1 vanilla pod, split and seeds scraped

To serve

125g blueberries

125g raspberries

125g blackberries

200g strawberries

juice of ½ lemon

75g caster sugar

For the babas, lightly butter 10 individual baba tins (or you can use dariole moulds); five will do if you bake the babas in two batches). Warm the milk to tepid. Sprinkle in the yeast and leave until dissolved.

Put the flour, salt and sugar into an electric mixer fitted with a dough hook and mix on a low speed for a minute.

Add the milk and yeast mixture, followed by the eggs, and mix on a low speed until you have a smooth dough. Now slowly add the soft butter and continue to mix until the dough becomes smooth and shiny.

Remove the bowl from the mixer and cover with cling film. Leave the dough to rise in a warm place for about an hour until it has doubled in size.

Turn the dough out onto a lightly floured surface and knock back gently. Divide the dough into 10 equal pieces, about 35g each, and roll into small balls. Place in the prepared baba moulds, cover with cling film and leave to prove in a warm place for 40–50 minutes until risen to the top of the tins.

Meanwhile, heat the oven to 180°C/Gas 4. Once proved, bake the babas for 12–15 minutes until deep golden. Turn them out onto a wire rack and leave to cool.

To make the whisky syrup, dissolve the sugar in the water in a large pan over a medium heat, then bring to the boil. Add the whisky to taste, vanilla seeds and citrus zests, then remove from the heat and allow to cool down slightly.

Add the babas to the warm whisky syrup and leave them to soak for about 1 hour, turning them every 10 minutes or so.

For the Chantilly cream, whisk the cream, icing sugar and vanilla seeds together in a bowl to soft peaks.

In a separate bowl, toss all the berries together with the lemon juice and sugar.

Put the babas into individual bowls, pour the whisky syrup over them and add the berries. Serve with the Chantilly cream.

CHOCOLATE & WALNUT BROWNIES.

This dessert is universally popular and always brings a smile to everyone's face. It's one where you have a spoonful and can't resist another one. The secret here is to make sure you don't overcook the mixture, as the brownies must remain soft and gooey in the centre. **Makes 12**

200g unsalted butter, in pieces
300g good-quality dark chocolate
  (at least 55% cocoa solids),
  chopped into small pieces
90g plain flour
¼ teaspoon sea salt
1½ teaspoons baking powder
3 free-range medium eggs
250g soft dark brown sugar
2 teaspoons vanilla extract
200g walnuts, chopped

Chocolate sauce
110ml double cream
50ml water
60g caster sugar
220g good-quality dark chocolate,
  chopped into small pieces

Heat the oven to 170°C/Gas 3. Line a 30 x 20cm baking tin with baking parchment.

Put the butter and 200g of the chocolate into a heatproof bowl. Place over a pan of gently simmering water until melted. Stir until smooth. Remove the bowl from the pan and set aside to cool slightly.

Sift the flour, salt and baking powder together into a bowl.

In another large bowl, whisk the eggs, brown sugar and vanilla extract together until slightly thickened. Fold in the melted chocolate mixture, then gently fold in the sifted flour until just combined. Finally, carefully fold in the chopped walnuts and remaining chocolate.

Spoon the mixture into the prepared baking tin, gently spreading it into the corners. Bake for 20–25 minutes, until nicely crusted on the top and still soft in the middle.

Leave the brownie in the tin for 10 minutes, then carefully transfer to a wire rack and allow to cool.

To make the chocolate sauce, pour the cream and water into a heavy-based pan and bring to a simmer. Remove from the heat and stir in the sugar and chocolate. Continue to stir until the chocolate is melted and the sauce is smooth.

Cut the brownie into squares and serve with the chocolate sauce and whipped cream if you like.

BASIC RECIPES

CHICKEN STOCK.

Makes about 2 litres

2kg raw chicken carcasses
3.5 litres water
½ leek (white part), trimmed, washed
   and roughly chopped
½ white onion, peeled and roughly
   chopped
2 thyme sprigs
1 bay leaf
5 white peppercorns
sea salt

Remove any excess fat from the chicken carcasses and roughly chop them up. Place in a large saucepan and pour on the cold water to cover. Bring to the boil, then lower the heat and simmer gently for 20 minutes, skimming frequently to remove impurities that float to the surface.

Add the chopped vegetables, herbs, peppercorns and a little salt. Simmer gently for a further 1½ hours.

Pass the chicken stock through a fine sieve into a bowl, allow to cool and then refrigerate until required. Remove any fat from the surface before using. This stock can be kept in the fridge for 3–4 days or frozen for 3–4 months.

FISH STOCK.

Makes about 1.5 litres

2kg white fish bones, such as sea bass,
   John Dory or sole
50ml olive oil
½ white onion, peeled and chopped
½ leek (white part), trimmed, washed
   and roughly chopped
½ fennel bulb, roughly chopped
2 thyme sprigs
1 bay leaf
5 white peppercorns
150ml white wine
2 litres water

Chop the fish bones into small pieces and rinse them under cold running water to remove all traces of blood. Drain in a colander.

Heat the olive oil in a large heavy-based saucepan over a medium heat. Add the onion, leek, fennel, herbs and peppercorns and sweat for 4–5 minutes to soften and lightly colour. Add the fish bones and cook for a further 2–3 minutes.

Add the white wine and let bubble to reduce right down. Pour on the cold water to cover and bring to the boil. Lower the heat and skim off any scum from the surface. Simmer for 20 minutes.

Remove the pan from the heat and allow the stock to rest for 10 minutes. Pass through a fine sieve into a bowl, allow to cool and then refrigerate until required. Remove any fat from the surface before using. This stock can be kept in the fridge for 2–3 days or frozen for 3–4 months.

LAMB STOCK.

Makes about 1 litre

2kg lamb bones
2 tablespoons olive oil
3 carrots, peeled and chopped
1 onion, peeled and chopped
1 fennel bulb, roughly chopped
1 bouquet garni (see right)
½ head of garlic (cut horizontally)
½ red pepper
1 teaspoon ground cumin
1 teaspoon fennel seeds
3 tablespoons tomato purée
100ml white wine
2 litres water

Heat the oven to 200°C/Gas 6. Put the lamb bones into a roasting tray and drizzle with 1 tablespoon olive oil. Roast for 20 minutes or until golden.

Meanwhile, heat a large heavy-based pan over a medium heat and add the rest of the olive oil. Add the carrots, onion, fennel, bouquet garni and garlic and sweat for 6–8 minutes. Add the red pepper, cumin and fennel seeds and cook for a further 1–2 minutes. Stir in the tomato purée and cook for 2 minutes.

Pour the white wine into the pan and add the roasted lamb bones. Pour on the water to cover the bones, bring to the boil and skim off any scum from the surface. Lower the heat and simmer gently for 3–4 hours.

Discard the bones and strain the stock through a sieve into a bowl. Allow to cool and then refrigerate until required. Remove any fat from the surface before using. This stock can be kept in the fridge for 3–4 days or frozen for 3–4 months.

BÉARNAISE SAUCE.

Makes about 250ml

50ml white wine vinegar
50ml white wine
5 peppercorns, crushed
1 shallot, peeled and finely sliced
5 tarragon sprigs, plus 1 teaspoon
  chopped tarragon
3 egg yolks
3 teaspoons water
150g clarified butter (see right)

Put the wine vinegar, white wine, peppercorns, shallot and tarragon sprigs into a small saucepan and bring to a simmer. Let bubble to reduce down until only 1–2 teaspoons liquor remains in the pan. Remove from the heat.

Add the egg yolks and water to the reduction and whisk over the lowest possible heat until the sauce starts to thicken; do not overheat or it may curdle. You may prefer to heat the sauce in a bain-marie (a bowl over a pan of simmering water) to reduce the risk of overheating.

Remove the pan (or bowl) from the heat and slowly whisk in the clarified butter. Pass through a fine sieve and then stir in the chopped tarragon.

MAYONNAISE.

Makes about 300ml

2 free-range medium egg yolks,
  at room temperature
1 teaspoon Dijon mustard
25ml white wine vinegar
250ml sunflower or vegetable oil
sea salt
squeeze of lemon juice

Put the egg yolks into a medium bowl with the mustard and wine vinegar and whisk together until evenly combined. Now slowly drizzle in the oil, whisking continuously as you do so to emulsify the mixture. Once all the oil is added you should have a thick, glossy mayonnaise. Season with salt and add a squeeze of lemon juice to taste.

CLARIFIED BUTTER.

150g unsalted butter

Put the butter into a heavy-based saucepan and melt very gently over the lowest possible heat. The milk solids will separate out and fall to the bottom of the pan. Carefully pour the pure clarified butter into a bowl, leaving the milk solids behind in the pan.

BOUQUET GARNI.

2 leek leaves, washed
handful of parsley sprigs
handful of thyme sprigs
1 bay leaf

Lay one leek leaf flat on a board, put the herbs sprigs on top and cover with the other leek leaf. Tie with kitchen string to secure and use as required. (Illustrated on page 55.)

INDEX.

Publishing director Jane O'Shea
Creative director Helen Lewis
Project editor Janet Illsley
Design Nicola Davidson and Jim Smith
Photographer Laura Edwards
Food for photography Tom Kitchin
Props stylist Polly Webb-Wilson
Production Aysun Hughes, Vincent Smith

This edition first published in 2015 by
Quadrille Publishing Limited, Pentagon House
52–54 Southwark Street, London SE1 1UN
www.quadrille.co.uk

Quadrille is an imprint of Hardie Grant
www.hardiegrant.com.au

Text © 2012 Tom Kitchin
Photography © 2012 Laura Edwards
Design and layout © 2012 Quadrille Publishing Limited

Cataloguing in Publication Data: a catalogue record for this book is available from the British Library.

ISBN 978 1 84949 740 4

Printed in China

ACKNOWLEDGEMENTS

I should like to thank all those who have contributed to this book:
My dear wife Michaela for supporting and helping me through yet another project.
Jane O'Shea and Helen Lewis at Quadrille for their enthusiasm and belief in my ideas.
Laura Edwards for her beautiful photography and for capturing our vision.
Polly Webb-Wilson for sourcing incredible props.
Janet Illsley for editing and fine-tuning me.
Roxanne Newton and Holly Napoli for typing recipes and chasing me.
Mandy Jones, my very talented pastry chef, and the entire team at The Kitchin.
Martine Carter and Stripe Communications for their continued support.
My wee boys Kasper and Axel for coming along to photo shoots on Sundays and Mondays.

PROPS CREDITS

Ceramics Adam Pottery www.adampottery.co.uk; Andrea Walsh www.andreawalsh.co.uk; Fursbreck Pottery www.applepot.co.uk; Highland Stoneware www.highlandstoneware.com; Jane Kelly www.kosmoid.net; Mansfield Studios www.mansefieldstudios.com; Patricia Shone www.patriciashone.co.uk; Scandi Living www.scandiliving.com; Sue Paraskeva www.sueparaskeva.co.uk

Glass Glasstorm www.glasstorm.com; Lindean Mill www.lindeanmillglass.co.uk

Cloth Anta www.anta.co.uk; Breanish Tweed www.breanishtweed.co.uk; Karen Rao www.karenrao.com; Madeleine Shepherd www.madeleineshepherd.co.uk; Moons www.moons.co.uk; Pickone www.pickone.co.uk; Volga Linen www.volgalinen.co.uk

Basketware Lisa Bech www.bechbaskets.net

Kitchenware Alessi www.alessi.com; David Mellor www.davidmellordesign.com

Cutlery and Silverware Design at Home www.designathome.co.uk; Kirsty Eaglesfield www.kirstyeaglesfield.co.uk

Wood Pete Hewitt www.petehewitt.com; Real Wood Studios www.realwoodstudios.com

Stone Edinburgh Marble www.edinburghmarble.com; Slate UK www.slate.uk.com